T0078019

DEMOCRACY
FOR THE HAITIAN CRISIS
IDEAS FOR POLITICAL REFORMS IN HAITI

ARCHANGE DESHOMMES

authorHOUSE

AuthorHouse™
1663 Liberty Drive
Bloomington, IN 47403
www.authorhouse.com
Phone: 833-262-8899

Published by AuthorHouse 03/22/2022

ISBN: 978-1-7283-6906-8 (sc)
ISBN: 978-1-7283-7064-4 (e)

Print information available on the last page.

This book is printed on acid-free paper.

CONTENTS

INTRODUCTION

Democracy for The Haitian Crisis is not the product of mere luck. It is, on the contrary, the result of reflections on the constant political turmoil facing Haiti, our beloved country.

In 2002, I met Archange Deshommes at Virginia State University. He was a computer science student, and I was an education major. Each time we ran into each other, we almost always had the same topic of conversation: What the Haitian intelligentsia can do to solve those political problems. We were obsessed with that topic, even after graduation. In 2008, six years later, I obtained a master's degree in public administration from Strayer University, and my thesis was Democracy and Despotism. In this work, I compared and contrasted public administration in a democratic and a despotic regime. Recently, that is, 12 years later, Archange has surprised me by announcing to me that Democracy for The Haitian Crisis was ready to be published, and I was to write its introduction.

Both Democracy for The Haitian Crisis and Democracy and Despotism offer solutions to the political problems of Haiti. The former offers reforms to make government more functional for the Haitian people; the latter, wise recommendations to legitimate political leaders wishing to establish or strengthen democratic governments in their countries.

Haiti is currently going through one of its worst crises. It is needless to say that <u>Democracy for The Haitian Crisis</u> is an opportune book to read at present. Furthermore, it is very encouraging to know that some of us are still concerned about our country and strive to find practical solutions to its political problems. Enjoy your reading!

Jean Alphonse St. Louis,
- **Bachelor in Political Science, Virginia State University, Virginia, USA**
- **Master in Public Administration, Strayer University, USA**
- **Language Teacher, Richmond Public Schools, Richmond, VA, USA**

PRAISE FOR DEMOCRACY FOR THE HAITIAN CRISIS

Political instability and corruption are the major factors of Haiti's underdevelopment. what to do to act on these factors and to get the country out of this acute and hopeless crisis? In this book, the elements of solutions which are proposed by Archange Deshommes are quite relevant and convincing that I invite you to read absolutely.
Baby Jonas Jean, former community development officer, American Red Cross delegation, Port Au Prince, Haiti

I was pleased to read the first draft of DEMOCRACY for the Haitian Crisis written by Mr. Archange Deshommes. I specialy enjoyed reading the author's proposal for necessary reforms in matter of police and decentralization in Haiti. As a Teacher and a member of the Bar Association of Port Au Prince, Haiti, I strongly recommend this book to anyone who would like to get a deeper understanding of the social, political and economic systems that currently exist in Haiti and the world.
Kely Tabuteau,
-lawyer, State University of Haiti, Port au Prince, Haiti

- Master in Education, Nova Southeastern University, Florida, USA
-Math Coach, Miami Dade County Public Schools

———— ✠ ————

I believe that, if any society or government is to exist, it must have a government that supports its people by way of inclusion. The government must believe in a sound political system where people must be able to elect their officials and they who are elected must represent the people's concerns. This is what a democratic society must embodies and this is what the book represents. The people of Haiti deserve this.
Eldridge Mitchell,
-University of Miami Alumni, Miami, Florida, USA
-Social Science Teacher, Miami Dade county Public Schools

———— ✠ ————

Through this book, Archange Deshommes exposes the disintegration of Haitian society and the failure of its elites incapable of orienting this nation, which nevertheless remains a reference in the history of humanity, towards progress. With all humility, he suggests possible solutions that could put the country on the path of development based on a careful analysis of the different political systems. It's a great civic contribution to grasp good.
Nocles Debreus, Editor at Journal Le National, Port Au Prince, Haiti

ACKNOWLEDGMENT

I would like to thank first and foremost God almighty, for the seed of intelligence and the many doors he has open in front of me, to make this book a reality. My late Father, Desilus Deshommes, a founding member of several Seventh Day Adventist churches in Nassau, Bahamas including Francophone SDA, would love to see his first son write a book. I would like to thank my mother, Mariette Francois for emphasizing the importance of education at an early age in my life. I would like to thank my wife Esther Bonnet Deshommes, who has given me two beautiful children: Jonathan Archange Deshommes and Shamaelle Esther Deshommes, for new ideas about this book. Finally, I would like to thank my friends and Teaching colleagues for their intellectual support for this book: Jean Alphonse St Louis, Webert Nathanael Charles, Nocles Debreus, Eldridge Mitchell, Kelly Tabuteau, Dr. Miderge Lafleur, Pastor Augustin Hilaire, Baby Jonas, Josue Bonnet and many more who have inspired me to write this book.

DEDICATION

This book is dedicated to the different elites (Intellectual, Political, Economic, Religious, Medical, Technological, sportive, cultural, Etc.) that are searching for a real solution to the Haitian Crisis. This book is also dedicated to the Haitian Diaspora and the Haitian People for their still standing spirit in spite of the problems and obstacles that have plagued the country for decades.

CHAPTER 1

A BRIEF HISTORY OF THE COUNTRY

The years of the Spanish

Before the Spanish arrived on the island of Saint Domingue or Haiti, the inhabitants were the Indians primarily the Taino people. It is believed that the Taino Indians were part of a larger Indian groups that dominated the Caribbean before the European Arrival. This group was called the Arawaks. It is believed that the Arawaks were from South America. The Spanish arrived on the Island with Christopher Columbus in 1492. At first, the Spanish were very friendly to the Indians and the Indians were very friendly to the Spanish. Meanwhile, the Spanish population grew on the Island and wanted labor. The Spanish later on forced the Indians into hard works. The Indians were not accustomed to the hard works forced on them by the Spanish and they died in great numbers. The Indians fought the Spanish to prevent the Spanish from enslaving them. Unfortunately for the Indians, the Spanish had better weapons and they prevailed in those fights and wars.

The Spanish brought the first group of slaves from West Africa to Saint Domingue in 1503. The Spanish brought the slaves to replace the Indians in the hard work that needed to be done in Saint Domingue. The blacks from West Africa were very strong to do the jobs that needed to do in Saint domingue and the Spanish masters loved that. Every now and then, there would be an uprising of slaves. The Spanish managed to keep the slaves under control and managed to make Saint domingue a prosperous colony for the mother country, Spain.

The years of the French

In the region called the Caribbean, there were constant hostilities between the Europeans colons to set colonies for their mother countries from Europe. The French Pirates and Buccaneers were constantly at war with the Spanish in trying to control Saint Domingue. In 1625, the French buccaneers settled in the Tortuga Island. That was a clear message to the Spanish that the wealth of Hispaniola is not going to go to Spain only but to France Also. In 1663, the French would settle a colony in Leogane, a city in the West Department of Haiti. As the French moved Eastward on the island, they forced the Spanish to give up lands. In 1664, the French West India company took over the eastern part of the Island to manage it for the benefit of the mother country, France. The French West India Company was a company that built colonies for the benefits of the mother country, France. To prevent wars and strife with the French, the Spanish ceded the western part of the Island to the French in 1697 by the treaty of Ryswick. With that treaty, the western part of the island was legally for France. The French built different cities all over the western part of the Island including Port de Paix and Cap-Francais which is Now, Cap Haitien.

Besides building cities, the French built on what the Spanish had left and made Saint Domingue one of the most prosperous European colonies in the world. The businesses of Tobacco, sugar cane, Indigo, cotton and cacao were booming beyond belief. That is why Haiti was known as the pearl of the Caribbean or the pearl of the entiles. While the economy of Saint Domingue was prospering, the slaves did not enjoy that wealth. They were very frustrated by that development. Every now and then, there would be a small revolt. The French would find a way to maintain peace and keep the slaves in slavery.

The years of revolution

The weakness of France to control the slaves in Saint Domingue started with its weakness in Europe. The French Revolution in 1789 made it very difficult for France to control what was going on in France and what was going on in the Caribbean particularly in Saint Domingue. In 1791, the slaves in Northern Haiti in what is now Cap Haitian started a revolution that would eventually lead Haiti to independence. Boukman, a voodoo priest, would start the Bois Caiman ceremony that gave the revolution its official beginning. Boukman, would be captured later on by the French forces. His head would be cut off by the Slaves masters. The death of Boukman and other rebels would not have the power to slow the progress of the Revolution. At the early stage of the revolution, some of the mulattoes were aligned with the French and were trying to fight to keep the slaves under control. When France realized that, it was about to lose the entire country, it wanted to free some slaves, in some parts of the country. The leadership of the Blacks: Toussaint, Dessalines and Christophe wanted freedom for all blacks not just some. They wanted a full scale revolution. The British who were already in the Caribbean took advantage of the weaknesses of the French at home and abroad to settle in Saint Domingue. They were not successful in doing so. Toussaint pushed them back off the island. Some of the British forces died also of diseases in Saint Domingue. In spite of the last effort by the French to recapture the control of the colony by French general Charles Leclerc, Toussaint Louverture set the stage by winning some of the most important battles for the independence of the country. After the capture of Toussaint, Dessalines Took over the leadership role. He fought the French forces at the battle of Vertieres in 1803 and declared Haiti an independent country in January 1, 1804.

The early years of Independence

Haiti or the land of mountains was now the first independent black republic in the world. Along with the United States, it is one of the oldest country in the western hemisphere. After the independence, even though there were damages done, Haiti was still the richest country in the Caribbean and one of the richest in the world. Right after independence, something happened. It was the death of Jean

Jacques Dessalines. That first assassination of a chief of State or that first coup d'etat would lead to a period of political instability that would last 200 years. Henri Chistophe did not trust the mulattoes and would set his kingdom in the north. Alexandre Petion would set the Republic of the South. Alexandre Petion tried to set a democratic system by land distribution. When he suspended the legislature in 1816, it was clear that the ambition of Petion was not democracy but the establishment of a dictatorship. He declared himself president for life with the right to name his successor. Before his death, he did exactly that. He named Jean Pierre Boyer, a military man as the next president of the country.

The years during and after president Jean Pierre Boyer

Jean Pierre Boyer replaced Alexandre Petion as president in 1820. He managed to unite the country under a single leader and brought the eastern part of the island under his control. Jean Pierre Boyer ruled the whole island for about 25 years. From 1824 to 1826, he welcomed the blacks or African Americans who were fleeing the harsh treatment of the Jim Crow system in the United States. By the way, the Jim Crow system was a series of laws that were passed to make the condition of the black man unbearable in the United States. Before Jean Pierre Boyer was ousted by a rebellion in 1843, the country suffered the massive Earthquake that was known as the 1842 Cap Haitian earthquake that killed more than 10 thousand people. One of the greatest achievements of President Boyer was his diplomatic skills in working with the French government to recognize Haiti as an independent country. He also worked with other countries such as the United States to create a friendly relationship. The Dominicans have been very critical of president Jean Pierre Boyer because they believe, he kept them in a state of social, political and economic retardation for decades. After the presidency of Boyer, a series of unstable and military governments would come to power and would eventually lead to the American Occupation. Charles Riviere Herard would set the stage for the Boyer's Coup d' Etat and would replace him in 1843. After Herard, a series of military men would lead the country in a state of political instability that would require outside intervention for peace.

The years of the American Occupation

President Jean Pierre Boyer managed during his years in office to create a culture of peace because of the stability of the government under his leadership. He was a dictator just like Petion, but he manages to maintain the peace of the country. When he left office in 1843, just like I said before, a series of unstable governments came to power that required an outside intervention. There were a lot of forced exiles and political assassinations all over the country. During these years, the German Empire was very strong and therefore was trying to be influential in the Caribbean. During the 1915, there was a growing community of Germans in Haiti who was interested in doing business in the country. The connection of that German community with mainland Germany, made the influence of the Government inevitable.

Since the Caribbean is America's backyard in a political sense, the United States did not want to see the Germans control Haiti and therefore was using any means necessary to prevent them from being an influence in the country.

On July 28, 1915, under the leadership of President Woodrow Wilson, the United States invaded Haiti to protect its interests, the interest of its friends and to prevent the German government from being too influential in the country. The United State would stay in Haiti for 19 years until the presidency of Franklin Delano Roosevelt. With the backing of the US marine corps, American politicians would govern the country in a way that was not beneficial for the majority of the people of the country. The US government dismantled the constitution to create a military dictatorship. This was an effort to govern the country in a more unilateral way, to prevent the Germans from making any decision that might lead to them jeopardizing American interest in the country. The Haitian people and the intellectual elite did not welcome the occupation and they started fighting it from day one. Mulattoes such as Phillipe Sudre Dartiguenave and Louis Borno accepted to be presidents during that occupation even though the intellectual elite and the people of Haiti were not for the occupation and did not want them to become presidents.

With these leaders, FDR managed to write a constitution that gave the international community more power in Haiti. The Power to buy land for example was granted to foreigners. That was something that Jean Jacques Dessalines did not want at all during his leadership of the country. Even before the end of the presidency of Woodrow Wilson in the United States, the occupation did not give the United States a good image in the international community. The peace conference in Paris in 1919 did not welcome the occupation. The great depression that was full blown under the leadership of president Herbert Hoover made its way to the presidency of Franklin Delano Roosevelt. Under Roosevelt, things were very chaotic in Haiti because of the resistance and the depression. On a visit to Haiti in 1934, the message of President FDR was clear: the occupation would be ended and a policy of good neighbor would be implemented between the United States and Haiti. President FDR ordered the marines to live Haiti on August 15, 1934. That was the end of the physical occupation of Haiti by the United States. The signs and the psychological effects of the occupation would go beyond the departure of the marines.

The years after the American occupation

Just like before the American occupation, a series of unstable government followed the end of the American occupation. What you have to understand here is the fact that, the historical enemy of the country was still there. I am talking about the armed forces of Haiti. You see, the enemy has never been only the foreign policy of the United States of America. The enemy has been the army or the armed forces of the country also. The same army that assassinated Jean Jacques Dessalines was the same army that was giving problem before the occupation and after the occupation. After the departure of the marines in 1934, a series of men became leaders of the country. Stenio Vincent, Elie Lescot,

Dumarsais Estime, Paul Magloire, and François Duvalier. President Vincent had a lot of challenges during his presidency. One of them was to deal with the dominican dictator Rafael Leonidas Trujillo Molina. That dominican dictator wanted to spread his influence over all Hispaniola just like Jean Pierre Boyer had done. He had killed or massacred over 20, 000 Haitians. Lack of support from the United States forced Stenio Vincent to hand power over to Elie Lescot in 1941. Elie Lescot was very anti-Marxist. After all, he would have been impossible for him to have the support of the United States as president and being pro-Marxist. His attacks on the Marxist intellectuals in the country forced his presidency to an end in 1956 because of protests all over the country by different sectors of the Haitian society. Elie Lescot was replaced in 1946 by Dumarsais Estime.

Unlike the other military leaders, Estime was a civilian. He was more for the people of the country than for a small group called the elite. Most of the mulattoes of the country were part of that elite. Dumarsais estime excluded the economic elite made mostly of mulattoes from the government and forced them to pay taxes. That move was not welcome by the economic elite that has controlled the government since the departure of Boyer. Because of popularity, Estime was trying to extend his term in office. He was ousted by the army in 1950. Paul Magloire replaced Estime as president in 1950 after the coup. He returned the economic elite in their previous leadership position by giving government jobs to his friends and the friends of his friends. The People of the country was not in agreement with the presidency of

Magloire because his policy was not good for the people. Protests in 1956 force him out of power.

The years of the Duvaliers

Francois Duvalier came to power after the fall of Paul Magloire as president. He was not a military man but a doctor. He was a doctor who was very popular among the people. Before becoming president, one thing Francois Duvalier had managed to do successfully, is not to trust the army. He was very anti-mulattoe and anti-intellectual.

Under his leadership, the intellectuals and the Mulattoes fled the country to the United States, Canada, France, Jamaica and other countries. He ruled the country for about 14 years and died in 1971. Even though his presidency had some progress when it comes to the rebuilding of the country, at the institutional level, it was nothing but a dictatorship. When Jean Claude Duvalier replaced his dad in 1971, he tried to continue what his father had started. It was politics in the name of the father and the son. The military was governing the country indirectly through Jean Claude. The uprising of the people and the intellectuals forced Jean Claude out of power in 1986 after 15 years of government.

The years after the Duvaliers

When Jean Claude Duvalier left power in 1986, he left the same army that Jean Jacques Dessalines left after his assassination in 1806. A CNG or Conseil National de

Gouvernement was formed to run the country. The United States, France and the intellectuals of the country have managed to give Haiti the 1987 constitution that still in use today. Intellectuals such as Leslie Francois Manigat, Marc L Bazin and others were very involved in the politics of the country with resistance movements outside of Haiti in the Haitian diaspora. Leslie Francois Manigat was president but for only a period of three months in 1988. Several governments have come and go between the presidency of Leslie Francois Manigat and the election that brought Jean Bertrand Aristide to power in 1990. That catholic priest was very influential among the people. His presidency would not last for long. The coup d'etat of September 30, 1991 forced him into exile. He would return to power in 1994 with the backing of the government of the United States. His former prime minister Rene Garcia Preval would replace him as president for five years. Aristide would come back to power after the presidency of Preval in 2001. He would be out of power by a coup d'etat in 2004. His government would be followed by a transitional government led by president Alexandre Boniface and prime minister Gerard Latorue.

The 2006 election brought Preval back to power for a second term in office. The 2010-2011 general election would bring musician Michel Joseph Martelly to the presidency of Haiti for a Five Year term after defeating the establishment candidate and reknown intellectual in constitutional law Mirlande Manigat, the wife of former president Leslie Manigat.

As you can see, the history of Haiti is full with trials and tribulations. In spite of these trials and tribulations, I sincerely believe progress can be made in a political manner. The 1987 constitution has been a step in the right direction. The influence of the army is no longer a major factor in the stability of the country, what we have to do now is to fix the constitution so the country can be moved from that constitutional period to an administrative period that will be good for all Haitians in all classes and of all skin colors.

CHAPTER 2

WHAT TYPE OF DEMOCRACY FOR HAITI?

In the news, among the common people, you hear the debate about Democracy. Educated people, politicians, etc. talk about democracy as one type of government. In a sense, this is true. If you look at the big picture about government, that is correct. When you look at the word Democracy deeper, there are different types that exist. Different countries have different cultures. The type of government that can exist in one country may not be able to exist in another country. Communist governments have failed in Western Europe but succeeded in SouthEast Asia and China. Why? It has a lot to do with the culture of the country. Semi Presidential government has succeeded in France and Failed in Germany where it first appeared in the early part of the 20th century. In the rebuilding process of Haiti, not understanding the type of democracy that is more suitable for the country is a big mistake and that is exactly the mistake made in the 1987 constitution and the 1987 amended constitution.

The three main Types of Democracy

Different types of governments have existed throughout human history. Dictatorship, Constitutional Monarchy, Absolute Monarchy, Theocracy, communist governments, Democracy, etc. All of these forms of governments have affected society one way or another. History has proven Democracy has the best impact on society when compared with the others. Invented by the intellectuals at the time of ancient Greece in Athens and developed by the Romans, Germans, French, British, Americans, etc. The word Democracy is defined as the government by the people and for the people. Democracy can be direct where the people vote for a president to defend their interest for example president Jovenel Moise. Democracy can be indirect where the people vote for a parliament to defend their interests that vote for a Prime Minister for example prime minister Laurent Lamothe.

There are three main types of democracy: Parliamentary democracy, semi presidential democracy and presidential democracy. This sentence right here is one of the most important sentence in this book. If you understand this, you will understand the current political crisis in Haiti. If you do not understand this, you will not understand the current political crisis in the country.

Semi Presidential Democracy

The semi presidential system or semi parliamentary system has its origin in the Weimar Republic in Germany from 1918 to 1933. It is 100 years old. This was one of the most difficult moment in the history of Germany. This system of government made it possible for Adolph Hitler to rise to power and open the door for the holocaust and the Second World War. After the allied occupation of Germany, the Germans change from a semi presidential system to a parliamentary system of government. The constitution of Germany in 1919 established the Semi-presidential system of government. The president was popularly elected for seven years and can be re-elected. He appoints the prime minister called the Chancellor. Along with the prime minister or the chancellor, the president can dissolve parliament or the bundestag. In case the Chancellor does not go with the plan of the president to dissolve parliament, he could be dismissed by the president to appoint a new Chancellor that would eventually do his dirty job for him. Whenever the president does not have a majority in parliament to help him run the country, the concept of calling for new election was a normal thing. Prime ministers or chancellors go as quick as they come and there was that culture of political instability in Germany.

Political scientists are just like engineers who build schools, bridges, government buildings, etc. They cannot assume that their construction will never fail in extreme conditions but they have to build them as sufficient as possible to resist natural and environmental pressures. If the semi-presidential system was used to resist societal conflicts such as different political ideology, conflicts of interests among different groups, it has failed miserably. The only way to fix the brokenness of Semi presidentialism is to innovate to a parliamentary system of government. Even though the French government has managed somewhat to make it work just like the American government has managed to make the presidential system work, smaller countries with no deep history of political stability will not be able to do so. If they do not innovate, they would have to face the disastrous consequences of Semi-presidentialism.

This system is organized where the people vote for a president in a direct election and parliament chooses a person to be prime minister in an indirect election to form a government of cohabitation between the president and the prime minister. Countries that use this system today are: Haiti, France, Russia, French speaking African countries such as Democratic Republic of Congo and others. According to researches made by the World Bank, Yale University and Legatum institute in the United Kingdom, this system is very unstable and create a lot of confusion. French speaking African countries and Haiti are perfect examples of this broken system. Many scholars use the French Fifth Republic to justify the Semi-Presidential system as a good government. The reality is different.

When studying France in an advance way, most of the politicians at the municipal level, departmental level and regional level are elected indirectly by city council or departmental council or regional council. The presidential candidates in France usually come from one of those council or have his or her root in local politics. That is very different in countries that do not have this strong local, departmental and regional governments. In those countries, Semi Presidentialism can do a lot of damages. Presidents in Semi presidentialism bypass parliament to call for referendum, they appoint prime ministers, other ministers and advisers based on their selfish personal ideology. In semi presidentialism, the opinion of one person becomes the politics of a nation. The vision or the lack of vision of one person become the destiny of the whole country. This is unacceptable.

Semi Presidentialism and the crisis in the Democratic Republic of Congo in the late 1990s

The origin of the political crisis in the democratic Republic of Congo has to do with the form of government that the politicians and the intellectuals set for the country in the constitution. That system is the semi presidential government. This system as explained before, is a recipe for disaster. Just like in presidential governments, all the power belongs to that person and his entourage or government. Mobutu Sese seko has been in power from 1965 to 1997.

During his time, he was an allied of the United States, France, Belgium and many other western countries. He was a politician way before becoming president. During his time in office there was a lot of corruption, the economy deteriorate severely and finally rebel forces led by Laurent Desire Kabila expelled him from office and from the country. He died months later in Morocco. During that uprising by Laurent Kabila, thousands of people were killed on both sides. The Kabila side and the government side.

Semi Presidentialism and the crisis in Haiti in 2004

Haiti just like the Democratic Republic Congo has a semi presidential system of government since 1987 when they enacted the first democratic constitution for the country. President Aristide was in office for the second time from 2001 to 2004. His entourage was getting richer and richer while the people of the country were getting poorer and poorer. People were getting killed left and right by people associated with Fanmi Lavalas, the party of president Jean Bertrand Aristide. Guy Phillippe led the uprising that removed Aristide from Power. He settled in the Central African Republic and later in South Africa. Former Haitian diplomat Gerard Latortue and supreme court leader Alexandre Boniface organized the interim government as president and prime minister.

Semi-Presidentialism and the 2011 civil war in Syria

Syria is a semi-presidential republic where the president is elected by popular suffrage and the prime minister is chosen by the president with the approval of parliament. The conflict in Syria is part of the Arab spring or the Arab uprising in countries with broken governments and broken institutions. The people of Syria were unhappy with the way president Bashar Al Assad was running the country and demanded his removal and the departure of the government. This conflict of interest led to a full blown war in Syria between government forces supported by Russia and Iran and the rebel forces supported by the United States and the European Union. As a result of the war, more than 500 thousand people have been killed since 2011, more than 7 million internally displaced and more than 5 million refugees.

Just like in Germany during the First World War and the Second World War, this semi-presidential system has a lot to do with this war. If Syria did have a parliamentary system or a regime of assembly, the possibility for the war would have been less and less. This semi-presidential system set by Germany during the years of the Weimar Republic in 1918 has been a recipe for disaster in countries with weak democratic traditions such as Haiti, countries in Africa and the Middle East.

A few other countries with the semi presidential system of government

Russia

Based on The Constitution of Russia, the country is a semi-presidential republic, where the President is the head of state and the Prime Minister is the head of government. The Russian Federation is fundamentally structured as a multi-party representative democracy, with the federal government composed of three branches:

Legislative: The bicameral Federal Assembly of Russia, made up of the 450-member State Duma and the 170-member Federation Council, adopts federal law, declares war, approves treaties, has the power to impeach the President of Russia.

Executive: The President is the Commander-in-Chief

of the Armed Forces, can veto legislative bills before they become law, and appoints the Government of Russia (Cabinet) and other officers, who administer and enforce federal laws and policies.

The president is elected by popular vote for a six-year term (eligible for a second term, but not for a third consecutive term). Ministries of the government are composed of the Premier and his deputies, ministers, and selected other individuals; all are appointed by the President on the recommendation of the Prime Minister. Leading political parties in Russia include United Russia, the Communist Party, the Liberal Democratic Party, and A Just Russia. In 2019, Russia was ranked as 134th of 167 countries in the Democracy Index, compiled by The Economist Intelligence Unit, while the World Justice Project, as of 2014, ranked Russia 80th of 99 countries surveyed in terms of rule of law.

Judiciary: The Constitutional Court, Supreme Court and lower federal courts, whose judges are appointed by the Federation Council on the recommendation of the President, interpret laws and can overturn laws they deem unconstitutional.

South Korea

The government of South Korea is determined by the Constitution of the Republic of Korea. Like many democratic states, South Korea has a government divided into three branches: executive, judicial, and legislative. The executive and legislative branches operate primarily at the national level, although various ministries in the executive branch also carry out local functions. Local governments are semi-autonomous, and contain executive and legislative bodies of their own. The judicial branch operates at both the national and local levels. South Korea is a constitutional democracy.

The constitution of South Korea has been revised several times since its first promulgation in 1948 at independence. However, it has retained many broad characteristics and with the exception of the short-lived Second Republic of South Korea, the country has always had a semi presidential system with an independent chief executive. Under its current constitution the state is sometimes referred to as the Sixth Republic of South Korea. The first direct election was also held in 1948. Although South Korea experienced a series of military dictatorships from the 1960s until the 1980s, it has since developed into a successful liberal democracy.

Portugal

Portugal has been a semi-presidential representative democratic republic since the ratification of the Constitution of 1976, with Lisbon, the nation's largest city, as its capital. The Constitution set the division or separation of powers among four bodies referred as "organs of Sovereignty": the President of the Republic, the Government, the Assembly of the Republic and the Courts.

The President of Portugal is elected to a five-year term, has an executive role. The Assembly of the Republic is a single chamber parliament composed of 230 deputies elected for a four-year term. The Government is headed by the Prime Minister and includes Ministers and Secretaries of State. The

Courts are organized into several levels, among the judicial, administrative and fiscal branches. The Supreme Courts are institutions of last resort/appeal. A thirteen-member Constitutional Court oversees the constitutionality of the laws.

Portugal has a multi-party system of competitive legislatures/local administrative governments at the national, regional and local levels. The Assembly of the Republic, Regional Assemblies and local municipalities and parishes, are dominated by two political parties, the Socialist Party and the Social Democratic Party, in addition to the Unitary Democratic Coalition (Portuguese Communist Party and Ecologist Party "The Greens"), the Left Bloc and the Democratic and Social Centre – People's Party, which gain between 5 and 15% of the vote regularly.

The Head of State of Portugal is the President of the Republic, elected to a five-year term by direct, universal suffrage. He or she has also supervision and reserve powers. Presidential powers include the appointment of the Prime Minister and the other members of the Government (where the President takes into account the results of legislative elections); dismissing the Prime Minister; dissolving the Assembly of the Republic (to call early elections); vetoing legislation (which may be overridden by the Assembly); and declaring a state of war or siege. The President is also Commander-in-Chief of the Armed Forces.

The President is advised on issues of importance by the Council of State, which is composed of six senior civilian officers, any former Presidents elected under the 1976 Constitution, five-members chosen by the Assembly, and five selected by the president.

CHAPTER 3

PRESIDENTIAL DEMOCRACY

The second system, is the presidential system of government. This system has its origin in the United States during the end half of the 18th century. This system is at least 200 years old. This system is set where two candidates for President and vice president campaign together. If they win the election they become president and vice president. Countries that use this system today include the United States, Mexico, Dominican Republic, Brazil, Argentina and others. A lot of intellectuals and politicians have been advocating for this system of government in the Haitian diaspora and in Haiti but according to research made by the world bank, Legatum Institute in the United Kingdom and Yale University department of Political science, this system is very broken and unstable. It makes possible corrupt and dysfunctional governments. The crisis in Venezuela, Honduras and the rise of president Trump to power in the United States are perfect examples of this broken system of government.

Despotism and authoritarianism are related to presidentialism. Once the president is elected, he might try to destroy his political opponents, dissolve parliament if he could and establishes a one- man show. The vision for the whole country is in the hand of just one person. Based on political scientists, the presidential system is constitutionally unstable to guarantee peace in the countries that it has been implemented. The situation in Latin America in the past has proved that over and over.

When the president is from one political party and another party control the legislature, this brings political instability with the presidential system. Presidents, governors, senators, deputies in a presidential system are not accountable to the people who voted for them because they have the tendency to blame each other for the problems they cannot resolve. Once the president is elected, it is very difficult to remove him from office. People have to wait for the next election. If the president has no vision, no experience and no learning ability while in power, the country will suffer for the duration of the presidential term. Even when a president is removed from office, his vice president will take over. This means little changes for the country.

Presidential democracy and the storming of the United States Congress in 2021

The United States of America has had this dysfunctional system of government for 200 years. Mayors, governors, city clerks, attorneys general, judges, presidents, etc. are elected directly by the people of the country. Even though multiple studies conducted by some of the country's most prestigious universities, including the political science department at

Yale and Havard universities, have concluded that reforms of the political system must be carried out as soon as possible. Politicians have ignored this harsh reality. Unlike political parties in Canada and France, the Democratic Party and the Republican Party have direct primaries. This means that the leaders or the national committees of these two parties do not choose the leaders to represent the parties in the elections, it is the locals who choose.

This is a very big problem. If the reforms had been made at least at the political party level, the 2021 riot would never have happened because someone like Trump would never have been president of the country. Instead of these politicians fixing their own broken political system, they are very busy selling it to the rest of the world and criticizing the system of other countries like the People's Republic of China.

Without proof, President Donald Trump claimed the 2020 election was stolen from him by Democrats for the wrong reasons and called his supporters to action. On January 5 and 6, 2021, thousands upon thousands of Trump supporters gathered in Washington DC and called on United States Vice President Mike Pence to reject Mr. Joe Biden's victory. On the morning of January 6, 2021, President Trump told his supporters already upset with the election result: "If you don't fight like hell, you won't have a country". Due to his confrontational language, thousands of his supporters marched inside the Capitol or Congress building where members of Congress were counted the Electoral College vote to formalize the victory for Biden. Protesters chanted: Hang Mike Pence. Capitol Police and DC Metropolitan Police tried their best, but were unable to prevent the crowds from entering Congress. As a result, five people were killed. A policeman and four demonstrators. Members of Congress had to flee for their lives, including the Vice President of the United States of America. The protesters caused a lot of damage to the offices of many members of Congress, including vandalizing the office of Nancy Pelosi who is the current president of the House of Representatives in 2021. If the United States of America had a regime of parliamentary government like Canada, Germany and Italy, that would never happen.

Presidentialism and the crisis in Honduras in 2009

President Manuel Zelaya was removed from office by the Honduran army based on a court order submitted by the supreme court of the country. He was first moved to Costa Rica and then later on to the Dominican Republic. The organization of American States, the United Nations and the European Union condemned the Coup d'Etat against Zelaya. Demonstrators supporting the coup and the demonstrators opposing the coup were marching all over the country. Ambassadors of Cuba, Venezuela and Nicaragua were detained and beaten by Honduran troops. It is believed that he was removed from office because he ignored the supreme court calling to cancel a referendum to rewrite the constitution of the country. President Barack Obama did not do much to support the return to power of president Zelaya even though he did not openly approve his ouster. After Zelaya, the US provided over 200 million dollars of aid to Honduras between 2009 to 2016.

Presidentialism and the crisis in Venezuela in 2002

President Hugo Chavez was elected in office in 1998. He planned to have a new constitution for the country which passed a referendum by more than 70%. His popularity and his friendship with Cuba among other things were not welcome by everybody. President Hugo Chavez was removed from power for about 2 days before returned to power by the people of Venezuela and trade unions. The moderate rank of the Venezuelan military played a key role in the return of the president to power. President Hugo Chavez appointed some people in his entourage in some important positions in oil companies and other key government positions. At least a million people were marching against that. The movement was organized by the opposition that is loyal to the United States, Canada and the European Union. Pedro Carmono, the director of the Venezuela chamber of Commerce was declared president of the Country. He dissolved parliament, the supreme court of the country and declared that the 1999 constitution is not valid. He was seen as a danger to the survival of Democracy in Venezuela by the people of the country.

A few other countries with presidential government

Mexico

Mexico or The United Mexican States are a federation whose government is representative, democratic and republican based on a presidential system according to the 1917 Constitution. The constitution establishes three levels of government: the federal Union, the state governments and the municipal governments. According to the constitution, all constituent states of the federation must have a republican form of government composed of three branches: the executive, represented by a governor and an appointed cabinet, the legislative branch or the congress and the judiciary, which include a state Supreme Court of Justice. They also have their own civil and judicial codes.

The federal legislature is the bicameral Congress of the Union, composed of the Senate of the Republic and the Chamber of Deputies. The Congress makes federal law, declares war, imposes taxes, approves the national budget and international treaties, and ratifies diplomatic appointments.

The federal Congress, as well as the state legislatures, are elected by a system of parallel voting that includes plurality and proportional representation. The Chamber of Deputies has 500 deputies. Of these, 300 are elected by plurality vote in single-member districts (the federal electoral districts) and 200 are elected by proportional representation with closed party lists for which the country is divided into five electoral constituencies. The Senate is made up of 128 senators. Of these, 64 senators (two for each state and two for Mexico City) are elected by plurality vote in pairs; 32 senators are the first minority or first-runner up (one for each state and one for Mexico City), and 32 are elected by proportional representation from national closed party lists.

The executive is the President of the United Mexican States, who is the head of state and government, as well as the commander-in-chief of the Mexican military forces. The President also appoints the Cabinet and other officers. The

President is responsible for executing and enforcing the law, and has the power to veto bills.

The highest organ of the judicial branch of government is the Supreme Court of Justice, the national supreme court, which has eleven judges appointed by the President and approved by the Senate. The Supreme Court of Justice interprets laws and judging cases of federal competency. Other institutions of the judiciary are the Federal Electoral Tribunal, collegiate, unitary, district tribunals, and the Council of the Federal Judiciary.

Brazil

Brazil is a democratic federative republic, with a presidential system. The president is both head of state and head of government of the Union and is elected for a four-year term, with the possibility of re-election for a second successive term. The President appoints the Ministers of State, who assist in government. Legislative houses in each political entity are the main source of law in Brazil. The National Congress is the Federation's bicameral legislature, consisting of the Chamber of Deputies and the Federal Senate. Judiciary authorities exercise jurisdictional duties almost exclusively. Brazil is a democracy, according to the Democracy Index 2010.

The political-administrative organization of the Federative Republic of Brazil comprises the Union, the states, the Federal District, and the municipalities. The Union, the states, the Federal District, and the municipalities, are the "spheres of government". The federation is set on five fundamental principles: sovereignty, citizenship, dignity of human beings, the social values of labor and freedom of enterprise, and political pluralism. The classic three parties branches of government (executive, legislative and judicial under a checks and balances system) are formally established by the Constitution. The executive and legislative are organized independently in all three spheres of government, while the judiciary is organized only at the federal and state and district spheres.

All members of the executive and legislative branches are directly elected. Judges and other judicial officials are appointed after passing entry exams. For most of its democratic history, Brazil has had a multi-party system, proportional representation. Voting is compulsory for the literate between 18 and 70 years old and optional for illiterates and those between 16 and 18 or beyond 70.

Together with several smaller parties, four political parties stand out: Workers' Party (PT), Brazilian Social Democracy Party (PSDB), Brazilian Democratic Movement (MDB) and Democrats (DEM). Fifteen political parties are represented in Congress. It is common for politicians to switch parties, and thus the proportion of congressional seats held by particular parties changes regularly. Almost all governmental and administrative functions are exercised by authorities and agencies affiliated to the Executive.

Chile

The current Constitution of Chile was approved in a national plebiscite—regarded as "highly irregular" by some observers—in September 1980, under the military dictatorship of Augusto Pinochet. It entered into force in March 1981. After Pinochet's defeat in the 1988 plebiscite, the constitution was amended to ease provisions for future amendments to it. In September 2005, President Ricardo Lagos signed into law several constitutional amendments passed by Congress. These include eliminating the positions of appointed senators and senators for life, granting the President authority to remove the commanders-in-chief of the armed forces, and reducing the presidential term from six to four years.

Chile has a presidential system of government where the president is elected for four years. The Congress of Chile has a 38-seat Senate and a 120-member Chamber of Deputies. Senators serve for eight years with staggered terms, while deputies are elected every 4 years.

Chile's congressional elections are governed by a binomial system that, for the most part, rewards the two largest representations equally, often regardless of their relative popular support. Parties are thus forced to form wide coalitions and, historically, the two largest coalitions (Concertación and Alianza) split most of the seats. Only if the leading coalition ticket out-polls the second place coalition by a margin of more than 2-to-1 does the winning coalition gain both seats, which tends to lock the legislature in a roughly 50–50 split.

Chile's judiciary is independent and includes a court of appeal, a system of military courts, a constitutional tribunal, and the Supreme Court of Chile.

CHAPTER 4

PARLIAMENTARY DEMOCRACY: THE ONLY LASTING SOLUTION TO THE CURRENT POLITICAL CRISIS IN HAITI

The third and last system is the parliamentary system of government. This system is at least 300 years old. This system has its origin in the United Kingdom during the early years of the 17th century. This system is characterized by the people voted for a parliament (senators and deputies) and the parliament choose a ceremonial president and the members of the chamber of deputies or the lower chamber form the government. Countries that use this system today include: the United Kingdom, Germany, Canada, Bahamas, Jamaica, South Africa, Trinidad and Tobago and many others.

According to research made by global institutions such as the world bank, Legatum institute, Yale University and many more, this system is the best system of government for countries that are ethnically, politically and ideologically divided. It is easier to pass legislation in a parliamentary system of government. Power is more evenly divided in different committees in parliament. Authoritarian president is almost impossible in this system. I have heard some people say that we have had a parliamentary system of government in the country, that has never been the case. We have had cases where the parliament chooses the President, that does not mean a parliamentary system of government.

I have been making social science research for the last 20 years, the parliamentary system has been very stable. Choosing this system of government will be the wisest decision of any politician or intellectual in Haiti. I have heard some people say the constitution has to be amended, this is true but we can start with presidential decrees and intellectual movements. At least 15 of the 20 richest countries in the world have parliamentary government. Parliamentarism is considered more flexible, allowing changes in legislations and policies as long as there is one party in majority in parliament or there is a coalition government. Politicians in a parliamentary system are more accountable and are more scrutinize.

The do nothing politicians found in the presidential system of government is very rare in the parliamentary system of governments. Since the elected deputy is also the member of the government, this person has the ultimate responsibility to deliver. Electoral districts found in parliamentary system tend to be smaller compared with a presidential system of government. The electoral district that voted prime minister Justin Trudeau to the Canadian parliament has a population of less than 150 thousand people in 2020. That makes Justin Trudeau more accountable to the people of that district. We know that he is the prime minister for the whole Canada but only a small district voted for him. In our beloved country

Haiti, large districts vote for senators, deputies, mayors, the president. That makes them less and less accountable to the people that they represent. Studies after studies have showed that the smaller the district, the more accountable is the politician of that district.

In France, there are municipal districts with less than 100 people. That makes the politicians more and more accountable. By the way, France has used the parliamentary model or regime of assembly for its decentralization laws of the 1980s. in a parliamentary system, the power is more evenly distributed in the different committees and commissions of parliament. In the presidential system, one man has all the executive power of the country in his hand. The prime minister in a parliamentary system cannot make the unilateral decision that presidents make in presidential system of government. Superstar politicians found in presidential republics are very rare in Parliamentary governments. Elections in parliamentary systems are more peaceful since the electors are not voting for a president in power but members of parliament. In France, the electors do not vote directly for the mayors, the departmental assembly presidents and the regional presidents. That makes the election more peaceful than countries such as Haiti where mayors, deputies, presidents, senators are elected directly by the people.

Countries such as Germany, Italy, Ethiopia used to have a presidential system of government or populist system of government now they have parliamentary system of government and they are way more stable. In Haiti, we cannot afford to stay with that semi-presidential system, it is more chaotic than we think. We have to do what the researches said we have to do which is adopting a parliamentary system as soon as possible.

Parliamentarism and the regime of assembly

The regime of assembly is when a country has a parliament with one chamber. The assembly has the legislative and the executive power at the same time. The Parliament of Israel, the national assembly of Panama, the parliaments of Greece, Sweden, Finland are unicameral or made of one chamber. I do not support this system for Haiti because of the absence of the senate. There is no check and balance with this system. We can use this regime of assembly at the municipal and departmental levels but not at the national level. Something similar to France at the municipal, departmental and regional levels and Canada at the provincial level.

A few other countries with the Parliamentary system of government

United Kingdom

The UK has a parliamentary government based on the Westminster system that has been copied around the world: a legacy of the British Empire. The parliament of the United Kingdom meets in the Palace of Westminster and has two houses: an elected House of Commons and an appointed House of Lords. All bills passed are given Royal Assent before becoming law.

The position of prime minister, the UK's head of

government, belongs to the person most likely to command the confidence of the House of Commons; this individual is typically the leader of the political party or coalition of parties that holds the largest number of seats in that chamber. The prime minister chooses a cabinet and its members are formally appointed by the monarch to form Her Majesty's Government. By convention, the monarch respects the prime minister's decisions of government.

The cabinet is traditionally drawn from members of the prime minister's party or coalition and mostly from the House of Commons but always from both legislative houses, the cabinet being responsible to both. Executive power is exercised by the prime minister and cabinet, all of whom are sworn into the Privy Council of the United Kingdom, and become Ministers of the Crown. For elections to the House of Commons, the UK is divided into 650 constituencies, each electing a single member of parliament (MP) by simple plurality. General elections are called by the monarch when the prime minister so advises. Prior to the Fixed-term Parliaments Act 2011, the Parliament Acts 1911 and 1949 required that a new election must be called no later than five years after the previous general election.

The Conservative Party, the Labour Party and the Liberal Democrats (formerly as the Liberal Party) have, in modern times, been considered the UK's three major political parties, representing the British traditions of conservatism, socialism and liberalism, respectively.

Japan

Japan is a unitary state and constitutional monarchy in which the power of the Emperor is limited to a ceremonial role. He is defined in the Constitution as "the symbol of the state and of the unity of the people". Executive power is by the Prime Minister of Japan and his Cabinet, whose sovereignty is vested in the Japanese people.

Japan's legislative organ is the National Diet, a bicameral parliament. It consists of a lower House of Representatives with 465 seats, elected by popular vote every four years or when dissolved, and an upper House of Councilors with 245 seats, whose popularly-elected members serve six-year terms. There is universal suffrage for adults over 18 years of age, with a secret ballot for all elected offices. The Prime Minister is the head of government and is appointed by the Emperor after being designated from among the members of the Diet. As the head of the Cabinet, the Prime Minister has the power to appoint and dismiss Ministers of State.

Historically influenced by Chinese law, the Japanese legal system developed independently during the Edo period through texts such as Kujikata Osadamegaki. However, since the late 19th century, the judicial system has been largely based on the civil law of Europe, notably Germany. In 1896, Japan established a civil code based on the German Bürgerliches Gesetzbuch, which remains in effect with post–World War II modifications. The Constitution of Japan, adopted in 1947, is the oldest unamended constitution in the world. Statutory law originates in the legislature, and the Constitution requires that the Emperor promulgate legislation passed by the Diet without giving him the power to oppose legislation. The main body of Japanese statutory law is called the Six Codes. Japan's court system is divided into four basic tiers: the Supreme Court and three levels of lower courts.

Italy, India and Israel

Italy has a parliamentary government based on a mixed proportional and majoritarian voting system. The parliament is perfectly bicameral: the two houses, the Chamber of Deputies with 630 deputies elected for about five years unless there is early election and the deputies meet in Palazzo Montecitorio, and the Senate of the Republic with 315 members elected for five years that meets in Palazzo Madama, have the same powers. The Prime Minister, officially President of the Council of Ministers (Presidente del Consiglio dei Ministri), is Italy's head of government. The Prime Minister and the cabinet are appointed by the President of the Republic of Italy and must pass a vote of confidence in Parliament to come into office.

The President of the Italian Republic is elected by an electoral college of about 1,000 members. It comprises both chambers of the Italian Parliament—the Chamber of Deputies and the Senate of the Republic—meeting in joint session, combined with 58 special electors appointed by the regional councils of each of the 20 regions of Italy. Three representatives come from each region (The only exception is Aosta Valley, which due to its small size only appoints one), so as to guarantee representation for all localities and minorities.

The Electoral College thus consists of: 630 deputies, 315 senators and 58 regional representatives.

According to the Constitution, the election must be held by a secret ballot, with the senators, deputies and regional representatives all voting. A two-thirds vote is required to elect on any of the first three rounds of balloting and after that a simple majority is enough. The number of rounds has often been large thanks to the secret ballot and fragmented nature of the Italian Parliament. The election is presided over by the President of the Chamber of Deputies, who calls for the public counting of the votes. The vote is held in the Palazzo Montecitorio, seat of the Chamber of Deputies, which is expanded and re-configured for the event.

The structure of the Italian judiciary is divided into three tiers: Inferior courts of original and general jurisdiction. Intermediate appellate courts which hear cases on appeal from lower courts. Courts of last resort which hear appeals from lower appellate courts on the interpretation of law.

In this chapter, it would be a mistake to forget India, the largest democracy and the largest parliamentary democracy in the world. One of the largest country in size, population and economy. The president, vice president, prime minister and other ministers are all chosen by parliament. This country has a well organized and functional justice system

Like India, Israel has a parliamentary system of government in which the president, prime minister and other ministers are chosen by parliament. Israel has the most democratic system of government in the Middle East. The parliament is unicameral, which means only one chamber. This model of a one-chamber parliament will not work well in Haiti because of the country's political culture. The judiciary system of Israel is well organized and functioning well.

Greece and Ethiopia

Greece is the cradle of democracy. Today, the country has a system of parliamentary government where the locals elect the unicameral parliament and the parliament chooses the president. The Government comes from within parliament. Its judicial system is well organized. Like Greece, Ethiopia has a parliamentary system of government based on the 1995 constitution. The Government comes from the House of People's Representatives or the Lower House. The president is chosen by parliament with limited power. The country has a well-functioning justice system.

CHAPTER 5

THE CONSTITUTIONAL PERIOD

I classified the history of Haiti into six main periods. You do not have to be in agreement with me because this is not a scientific fact. It is just the way I understand the country. For example, you can classify Haiti's history into as many periods as you want. As long as you can give logical explanation for that, it will not be a major problem. The six periods that exist in Haitian history according to my knowledge is: Slavery, division, American Occupation, Duvalier Dictatorship, the Constitution and Administration.

In this chapter I deal precisely with the constitutional period or what I call the constitutional crisis. We have crossed four periods already and that is political progress. A lot of people do not agree that we have made progress politically because they are looking at the economy not our political history. We have ended slavery by declaring Haiti an independent nation in January 1, 1804. Thanks to founding fathers such as: Toussaint l'Ouverture, Jean Jacques Dessalines and Henri Christophe. Right after Independence, the country was divided into two: North kingdom and South Republic.

Henri Christophe was the head man in charge of the North Kingdom and Alexandre Petion was in charge of the South Republic. With President Jean Pierre Boyer, the country was unified as one Republic. In 1815 because of political turmoil in the country, we were subject to the American Occupation. The American occupation ended in 1934.

A few years after the Occupation, President Francois Duvalier was elected president and later on president for life. That was the beginning of the Duvalier dictatorship. The Duvalier dictatorship ended in 1986 with the departure of Duvalier Jr. or Jean Claude Duvalier for France. In 1987, a new constitution was ratified and set a semi-presidential system of government in the country. The semi-presidential system of government set by the constitution in the country has not been successful.

The Haitian intellectuals that drafted the 1987 constitution has missed a golden opportunity to create a better Haiti and put us in our last period which is the Administrative period. People blame countries such as the United States and France for the constitution of 1987. The fact of the matter is that: They did not force the constitution on the political elite of the country. They have made a choice to create for themselves and for the people of Haiti a system of government that cannot be successful in a country such as Haiti. The country is too divided for a semi-presidential system of government to have good result.

If you notice, I do not mention the army as part of the problem. The reason for that is the fact that the army has been the problem ever since the assassination of Jean Jacques Dessalines to the presidency of Jean Bertrand Aristide. If for example, the political elite did form a parliamentary system of government in the 1987 constitution, it would be more difficult for the army to overthrow the government since the government would be inside parliament not in the hands of one person called the president. History has proven that military governments do not work. There might be a little success here and there but basically military governments all over the world have been nothing but failures. The simple reason for that is the fact that the military has never been trained to lead the country but to fight against invaders invading the country. As a matter of fact, history has proven that military government is the source of political instability in most of the unstable countries in the world.

The 1801 constitution

Together, a total of 23 constitutions have been proclaimed in Haiti. Just like I mention above, one of the main reason why these constitutions have never had a serious impact on the country is because of military regimes. As a matter of fact, military regimes were the main reason why we have had so many constitutions in Haiti. The 1801 constitution was known as Toussaint Louverture constitution. The constitution named Toussaint governor for life and gave him rights to name his successor in leading the government of the country. Toussaint Louverture was the main leader of the Haitian revolution. That successful revolution made Haiti the first independent black republic in the world and shook the institution of slavery all over the New world that comprised

North, Central, South Americas and the Caribbean. Toussaint was born in Cap Haitian in the Breda plantation.

It is believed that Toussaint godfather helped him with his education. As far as his family was concerned, Toussaint was married with Suzanne Simone Baptiste Louverture and Had several children. One of the most well-known of Toussaint children is Placide. Haitian historians believed that he was the eldest son. When it comes to religion, Toussaint was a devout catholic and was not in support for Voodoo. Some historians believe that is why Catholicism has had a such impact on the country way after Toussaint's Death. Toussaint first alliance in Saint Domingue was with the French against the Spaniards who were trying to control the Island. After the French and the Spanish found a way for peace in Saint Domingue, the political game had changed. The relationship between Toussaint and France has deteriorated to the point that Toussaint aligned himself fully for the black cause in Saint Domingue.

In 1801, France's goal was to give Saint Domingue a constitution that would perhaps re-institute slavery on the island. Toussaint made the smart step in drafting a constitution that would make Saint Domingue independent of French Laws. The constitution made it clear that all races and all colors are equal under the law.

Toussaint promoted the Roman Catholic Faith over voodoo as the state religion of Haiti. The French resisted the constitution because they wanted to re-institute slavery on the Island. The French claimed that the constitution did not make room for them in trading with Saint Domingue. They claimed that their officials were excluded from the government. Toussaint was betrayed by Jean Baptiste Brunet, a French general. He died in France of brain disease. The constitution of Toussaint or the 1801 constitution was a starting point in the struggle for a democratic Haiti.

The 1805 constitution

The constitution of 1805 was also known as the Jean Jacques Dessalines constitution. That constitution banned white from holding land in Haiti and declared freedom of religion. Unlike the constitution of 1801 that recognized the Roman Catholic Church as the state religion of the country, that constitution made it clear that people were free to practice voodoo or Roman Catholicism. Jean Jacques Dessalines was born in the North Department of Haiti in the commune of Cornier. He was born in slavery and was raised as an army officer under Toussaint Louverture. He joined the slave rebellion of 1791. His tactics in fighting for freedom gained him popularity and respect from all the blacks including Toussaint. He led many successful engagements including the captures of Haitian cities such as Jacmel, Petit Goave, Miragoane and Anse A veau.

Dessalines was very famous for burning entire villages where slave owners used to live. Dessalines is famously known for defeating the French forces sent by Napoleon under the leadership of general Charles Leclerc in the battle known as Crete-A-Pierrot. Charles Leclerc would later on die of yellow fever and be replaced by General Rochambeau of France. Jean Jacques Dessalines would later defeated Rochambeau and the French troops in the battle of Vertieres.

That final battle would set the stage for Dessalines to declare independence on January 1, 1804. Jean Jacques Dessalines led the only successful slave revolt in the history of black people on the entire earth. It was after that independence that the constitution was drafted. The constitution made him emperor for Life and other people were not happy about that. He was betrayed by people he thought were his friends.

The death of Dessalines made way for a new leader and therefore a new constitution. The death of Dessalines would eventually start a chain reaction of constitutions after constitutions as the leadership of the country changes as day and night until the presidency of Jean Pierre Boyer.

The 1807 Constitution

The constitution of 1807 recognize the North as a state or the Nothern State. The constitution recognizes Henri Christophe as the King of the north. Just like the constitution of 1801, Catholicism was recognized as the main religion or the only official religion and divorce among married couple was discouraged. Some Believe that Henri Christophe was born in the country of Grenada. Some people believe that he was born in Haiti. Regardless where he was born, he was a founding father of Haiti. During the Haitian Revolution, he fought under Toussaint Louverture who promoted him general. With Toussaint and Dessalines, he was very successful in fighting the French, Spanish and the British. After Toussaint was captured and sent to France, he sided himself with Dessalines in the fight for Independence of Haiti.

After Haiti's independence, it was not clear how the country would be governed since the mulattoes and the Blacks were in distrust among themselves. After the assassination of Dessalines, Christophe withdrew himself to the North. He did not trust Alexandre Petion or the other mulatto leaders. In 1805 Christophe invaded the Dominican Republic under the order of Jean Jacques Dessalines to defend the blacks that were living on that part of the Island. The French soldiers were killing and mistreating blacks severely on that side of the country. That invasion was not that successful but clearly sent a message to the French Soldiers there. As the president of the North kingdom, Christophe with his new constitution managed to build the massive Citadelle Laferriere. He managed to have good relationship with the United States and good trade relation with the British Empire.

The British agreed with Christophe not to import any new slaves in the Caribbean and Christophe agreed with the British not to threaten its colonies in the Caribbean. During that time, the French and the British were at war and Christophe sided himself with the British against the French. The 1807 constitution gave president Christophe enough power to make the North very prosperous. As a matter of Fact, the North was more prosperous than the South Republic controlled and organized by president Alexandre Petion. As far as Christophe was concerned, the mulattoes were the domestic enemies of the Black and did not want them in his government in the North. His constitution or the 1807 constitution did not make any provision to accommodate the mulattoes in the North. The constitution made it illegal for white to own lands in the North and the Mulattoes could not be part of the government.

The 1816 constitution

The constitution of 1816 was a revised version of the 1806 constitution. It was known as the Petion constitution. It created a bicameral Parliament and established Alexandre Petion as the president until his death. The members of the senate in Petion constitution was not elected by the people of Haiti but by the lower chamber or the chamber of Deputies. The members of the chamber of Deputies had to follow the list submitted by president Petion. It was not like they were free to elect anyone they wanted to elect. That constitution was modeled on the previous constitutions such as Toussaint's constitution in 1801 and Christophe's constitution in 1807.

That constitution gave citizenship to anyone live in the South Republic after 1 year of residence. Alexandre Petion was born in Port Au Prince from a White father and a black mother. He fought against the British invasion of the Island of Saint Domingue. Petion first allied with the French. After the deportation of Toussaint, He realized that the French wanted to re-institute slavery on the island and he aligned himself with Dessalines for the fight against the French. Just like before, after the Haitian independence, there was tensions between the Blacks and the Mulattoes and Petion aligned himself with the mulattoes.

It is believed that Petion had something to do or he was part of the assassination of Jean Jacques Dessalines. In Petion's part of the country or the South Republic. He seized land from wealthy land owner and distributed it to his supporters and the poor people of the country. They called him the good heart father or papa bon ke. Petion was a firm believer in Education.

He was respected for starting Lycee Petion which is a famous public school in Haiti under the control of the government. In 1815, he welcomed Simon Bolivar in Haiti and helped him in his fight for Independence in South America. Under Petion, Haiti helped countries such as Venezuela and others in their fight against European rules. The 1816 constitution lasted beyond the presidency of Alexandre Petion. After the death of President Petion of Yellow fever in 1818 and suicide by King Henri Christophe in 1820, Jean Pierre Boyer became president and used the 1816 constitution during his administration. Under the 1816 constitution, Jean Pierre Boyer United the North Kingdom and the South Republic into one nation.

He later on invaded the eastern part of the Island known as Saint Domingue and ruled the entire island for a period of 25 years. That constitution would be replaced by a new constitution known as the 1843 constitution after Jean Pierre Boyer left power with president Charles Riviere Herard.

The 1843 constitution

During the presidency of Charles Riviere Herard, Haiti has this constitution called the 1843 constitution. In this constitution, the judges were to be elected by the people instead of being appointed by the president. President for life was abolished. The office of the president was for four years. The parliament was conferred the power to make laws for the country. It was imperative that the army follows the law of the land.

The 1964 constitution

This is Francois Duvalier's constitution. That constitution would set the state for what I call the Duvalier Period. President Francois Duvalier became president in 1957. He was born in Port Au Prince and was also raised there. He attended the University of Haiti and became a doctor. He was very famous in fighting diseases such as Malaria. President Francois Duvalier saw the turmoil caused by the American Occupation. He witnessed the political instability that followed after the departure of the last US Marines in Haiti in 1934. He was a fervent follower of the Negritude Movement started by renown Haitian intellectual Jean price Mars. That movement was a philosophy for the emancipation of Blacks from French rules all over the world.

President Francois Duvalier entered Politics in the government of president Dumarcais Estime in 1946. The president appointed him the director of public Health and labor. That position would give Duvalier the voice he needed to make himself famous or popular in the country to later on becoming president for life. The 1957 presidential election was the perfect timing for Duvalier. All the balls were on his side of the field. Francois Duvalier had only two opponents in that election: Louis Dejoie, a rich mulattoe and Daniel Fignole, a government bureaucrat under Dumarcais Estime and provisory president of Haiti after the presidency of

Dumarcais Estime. Francois Duvalier defeated Louis Dejoie by letting the people know that he was mulattoe and the mulattoes have been responsible for the misery of the black population.

Since the blacks outnumbered the mulattoes, it was an easy win for Duvalier. Francois Duvalier defeated Louis Dejoie in the election and Daniel Fignole was forced to live the country against his will. He adopted a new constitution in 1957 to make room for him as the sole person in power in 1957. The army was not happy with the new constitution and tried to overthrow Francois Duvalier in a Coup. The coup was unsuccessful and the president killed a lot of military leaders and made major changes in the army to serve his personal interest and the interest of his friends. Exiled Haitians along with a few americans tried covert operations to overthrow the government and was very unsuccessful in defeating Francois Duvalier and his new constitution.

With that new constitution, Francois Duvalier solidified his power in all institutions of the country. He supported Voodoo over the Catholic Church that has been the state religion under past governments including under Toussaint Louverture. With more and more power, Duvalier made some changes in his 1957 constitution. He reduced parliament from two chambers to one. He was the only candidate in the election of 1961. In 1964 he had a constitutional referendum that made him president for life. He wanted to be president for life, he was president for life. He died in 1971 under the 1964 constitution that he wrote for his personal gain and the gain of his family and his friends.

The 1987 constitution

The Duvalier's constitution of 1964 was unaccepted to the people of Haiti, the intellectuals in the country and the International community. President Duvalier was not easy to remove internally or internationally. He was smart enough not to trust the army but created his own army or the tonton Makouts. The Tonton Makouts was ready to commit any kind of crime for Duvalier. Do not forget that the country had had a military government since the assassination of Jean Jacques Dessalines. The military appointed presidents and dismissed presidents as they wish. To run a country in the presence of a such military, someone had to be very smart. He had to be very smart at least in consolidating power. Francois Duvalier was that type of person. After the departure of Jean Claude Duvalier for France in 1986, the stage was set to have a new constitution.

The only problem in creating that constitution was the fact that, Duvalier Jr was gone but the army that has terrorized the country in the early days of the republic was still there. The 1987 constitution set a semi-presidential system of government. The president would be elected for a period of five years with no consecutive terms. That constitution did not allow for double citizenship. The parliament was made of two chambers. The judges of the supreme court would be appointed by the president himself. With the military culture of the country, the constitution was not respected. That semi-presidential system was not the best for a country as politically divided as Haiti.

As a result, a series of unstable government came to power

until the 1990 election that elect Jean Bertrand Aristide as the first democratically elected president of the Country. Others believed that professor Francois Manigat was the first democratically elected president of the country. This subject is a matter of debate. One thing is for certain, Jean Bertrand Aristide was extremely popular in 1990. He was very popular primarily among the poor. That constitution was not able to prevent the Coup D'Etat of September 30, 1991 against president Jean Bertrand Aristide. The army would take power and just like they have done for over 150 years, they set a military government under the leadership of Joseph Raoul Cedras. President Jean Bertrand Aristide would return in Haiti in 1994 under the Backing of the United Nations and the Clinton Administration.

At his return, president Aristide would dismantle the army that had caused terror in Haiti from the assassination of Jean Jacques Dessalines to the September 30, 1991 Coup against a democratically elected president. President Aristide believed the dismantling of the army has been the greatest success of his administration. I believe the same thing. President Joseph Michel Martelly has published the amended version of the 1987 constitution. I welcome the notion that 30% of all government jobs must go to women. With this little success, the major problems are still there. A parliamentary system of government should be set in motion at the national level.

While it was urgent to amend the constitution and to publish the amended version, like I said, the major problems are still there. That is why I believe that we are still in a constitutional crisis or a constitutional period.

The constitutional Period and the Elites of the Country

A country functions just like the human body with a lot of parts: the head, the yes, the neck, the heart, etc. All these parts make us human. If one part does not work, the whole body is sick. It is the same thing for any society including ours, Haiti. I had the chance to work as a public school teacher and also I had the chance to work in some private companies. It was the same thing. These corporations or the public school have different departments. If one does not work, the whole corporation or the whole school is handicapped. A country is made up of different groups of think tank called Elites. If one does not take its responsibility, the whole country cannot function well.

Intellectual, political and economic elites

The Intellectual elite is defined as a small group of educated people that are specializing in criticizing society in their field of expertise to make things better by proposing new ideas. This is the first elite, the ultimate elite. If one group of people has to be blamed for the predicament of Haiti, it has to be this group. In Haiti, there is a tendency to look at the intellectual elite as a group of University professors, Social science professors, or political scientists, historians, Economists or journalists. The truth is, the group is much larger than that. A musician or a soccer player can be part of the intellectual elite as long as he is or she is educated enough in his or her field of study and want to make changes for the betterment of the whole country.

The political elite is defined as a small group of elected officials or appointed officials that represent the people or the interest of the people in government or in politics. The mayors, the departmental delegates, the deputies, senators, ministers, presidents, etc. are all part of the political elite. Even though the political elite get their power from the people, they receive their assignments from the intellectual elite. We are in a constitutional crisis in Haiti and this constitution was written by the intellectual elite not necessarily by the politicians themselves. The intellectual elite is the engineer of the car while the political elite is the mechanic man of the car. The mechanic man cannot go beyond what the engineer of the car has allowed him to do. For the last 30 years, Haiti has had bad governments not only because of corrupt politicians but also because of bad ideas proposed by intellectuals in the constitutions.

The economic elite is the business men and business women, new entrepreneurs that are more interested in developing the country economically than in politics and academics. The economic elite can be local Haitians, Haitian in the diaspora, foreigners that are more interested in investments for a profit. While searching to better themselves financially, they create employment opportunities and develop the country physically. Just like the human body, if the intellectual elite and the political elite are broken, this elite cannot do its job. They are all related. Intellectuals and politicians in Haiti have the tendency to blame the bourgeoisie, the international community for their problem while they are not doing their parts. It is pure hypocrisy. In this constitutional period or constitutional crisis, the economic elite has to make their proposition for the betterment of the country.

Religious and Medical Elites

Different religions are present in Haiti. They are all helping the country spiritually and socially at least in their own eye. In this article I am not going to get into the theology of religion why this one is good and that one is bad. Why this one is going to take us into heaven while that one is going to take us into hell. I am not going that route. Here I am focusing more on the churches: Catholic, Pentecostals, Baptists, Seventh Day Adventits, etc and their social impact. I have been living in the USA for the last 20 years where the social impact of the churches are less and less relevant. As a result, the family and marriages are more and more disorganized and the whole country is paying the price. Compared with the USA, the religious elite has had a more positive impact in Haiti for the last 30 years. No other institution can keep the family together, preach morality, organized education as good as the churches. This elite should make its proposals for a better constitution for the country.

Dr. Jerry Batar was kidnapped and later on released by gang members in Port au Prince, Haiti in March 2020. While he was kidnapped, the whole hospital, Bernard Mevs Hospital, where he works along with nurses and other health care professionals was shut down and they were marching and demanding his immediate release. It is believed that he was kidnapped so he can help treat a famous gang member that was injured or becoming sick. When they finally released him, the hospital Bernard Mevs staff received him as a president. In the early 1990s, I was sick and I attended L'Hopital General for a few months. They did their best to help me. The medical elite just like the other elites is key for a better Haiti. They cannot do their work if the politicians and the social intellectuals are not doing their jobs. In Dr. Jerry Batar kidnapping case, President Jovenel Moise said the gang members have to take conscience. They are not going to take conscience. The political system must be reorganized to prevent these animal acts from taking place. This elite has a role to play in the political crisis or the constitutional crisis of the country.

Scientific and Technological elites

I grew up in Port au Prince arrondissement of Haiti, in the city of Delmas. Everywhere you go in Haiti, if I recall well, there was what they called: Ecole informatique or ecole science informatique or computer school. Sometimes, the school has 5 students. They have their nice looking uniforms on and a nice valise or professional bag and ready to learn. The Haiti Tech Summit that brings: Facebook, Google, AirBnB, Twitter, Amazon, etc to Haiti in the last 3 years is a great initiative. Science and technology have united the world and turn it into a small community. These corporations are on fire and ready to help rebuilding Haiti. They have the knowledge and they have the money. With a country in political crisis, their work is handicapped somewhat. They have to get involve in creating a better government for the country.

Sportive and cultural elites

Covid-19 closes all sports and cultural activities around the world in 2020. It's the same in Haiti. The sporting and cultural figures of the country can always give their support to the Haitian people through the Technological Paths (Facebook, Twitter, TV, Youtube, etc.) Emmanuel Sanon or Manno Sanon, one of the best Haitian footballer put Haiti on the global map during the 1974 World Cup in Italy because of his two goals against the famous Italian goalkeeper Dino Zoff. Zoff was very famous for his experience as a goalkeeper for the Italy team. Ronald Agenor was among the top 25 tennis players in the 1990s. Recently, I discovered a list on Wikepedia of the 100 great Haitian painters. Haitian actors like Languichate Debordus, Jesifra, Bisha, etc. have made a huge contribution to Haitian culture. Actors like Ronald Dorfeuille (Pyram), Jean Gardy Bien Aime, musical groups like Tabou Combo, Tropicana, Septentrional, Yole de Rose, Ancy de Rose, Neymours Jean Baptiste, Manno Charlemagne and the list goes on.

They have contributed enormously to the development of the country through music, sport, painting, cinematography, etc. This elite and the other elites not mention in this chapter have to get involved in creating a better government in Haiti.

The constitutional period and the Haitian army

The 1995 dissolved Haitian army by former president Jean Bertrand Aristide had its roots in the early days of the Haitian revolution when the former slaves led by Jean Jacques Dessalines, Toussaint L'ouverture, Alexandre Petion, Francois Capois ou Capois lamort, Henry Christophe, Magloire Amboise, Dutty Boukman and many others organized themselves to create the indigenous army of Haiti in the early days of the Reuplic. The indigenous army fought many famous battles including battle of Croix des Bouquets, battle of Gonaives, Battle of Jean Rabel, battle of Crete a Pierrot, Battle of Ravine a couleuvres, Battle of Saint Raphael, Battle of Vertieres where Haiti defeated the forces of Napoleon of France and become the first independent black republic in the world on January 1, 1804.

During the American Occupation from 1915 to 1934, the United States government disbanded the Haitian army to create the Haitian constabulary or La gendamerie d'Haiti. La Gendammerie D'Haiti was very involved in road constructions, health services and organized training to make it work better. The Gendammerie became the Garde d'Haiti in 1928. The Garde d'Haiti was the main force of the Haitian army after the United States occupation ended in 1934.

During the Francois Duvalier dictatorship in 1957, a strong control was put on the Haitian army. Duvalier himself did not trust the Garde d'haiti that was why he created les tontons macoutes or volontaires pour la securite nationale d'haiti. Francois Duvalier had executed many officers of the Haitian army.

After decades of interference in Haitian politics including many coup d'etats such as : the 1958 and 1963 coups d'etat attempt against Francois Duvalier and the successful Coup d'etat on September 30, 1991 against president Jean Bertrand Aristide, the Haitian army ceased to exist in 1995 after an executive order by President Jean Bertrand Aristide. During president Jovenel moise administration from 2017 to 2021, the army was rebuilt with the help of the Republic of Ecuador with a small force of about 500 soldiers.

Most people in Haiti are for the country to have a strong army. All the articles that create the army are still in the 1987 Haitian constitution. With good political reforms in the government to prevent or make it impossible for the army to do coup d'Etats, a strong regional army in Haiti will be a great thing. The army has had a great history in the days of the first battles for independence of the country.

CHAPTER 6

THE POLITICAL PARTIES

When it comes to political parties in Haiti, the history is not positive. Unlike our neighbors in the Caribbean, we do not have a stable history when it comes to the organization of political parties. In Jamaica for example, the present day People's national party has been in existence since 1938. The Jamaican labor party has been in existence since 1943. In the Bahamas for example, the progressive liberal party was founded in 1953 and the FNM or the Free National Movement was founded in 1971. These two countries mention here used to be colonies of Great Britain. This means that, they were not allowed to form political parties when the British government was in charge. These countries have proven that they are better in creating political stability than us in Haiti.

We can take the United States or Canada for example. In both countries, the history of political parties has been long, strong and a good example for people to follow in creating stable government. The democratic party in the United States started as early as 1830. The republican party also started early in American politics. If I am not mistaken, the Republican party goes back to 1854. If we go to the Canadians, we will find the exact same thing. The history of the liberal and conservative political parties in Canada goes back to the early and mid-19th century. What about our neighbor Dominican Republic? In the Dominican Republic, the history of political parties goes back to the mid-20th century. The social Christian Reformist party, the Social democratic Dominican Revolutionary Party and the Dominican Liberation party are well known all over the country.

What about France? Well, even though the history of political parties in France is not as stable as the history of political parties in the United States and Canada, the situation is not as bad as the one that we have in Haiti. The socialist party of France was founded in 1969 and the Union for a popular Movement or UMP was founded as a merger of different political parties in 2002. Just like the United States and Canada, France has a history of political stability. That means, we have countless of examples to follow when it comes to organizing political parties in Haiti. These countries, whether in the Caribbean or in North America or Europe, they are ready to help us. Let me make a bold statement: Organizing political parties is so simple, we can do it ourselves. All we have to do is to look at these countries as examples and copy the right things that they have done when it comes to organizing political parties and rejecting the bad things. It is that simple.

History of political parties from 1870 to Jean Claude Duvalier

The history of political parties goes back to the second half of the 19th century. To be precise, I can say that the history of political parties goes back to the last quarter of the 19th century. This is very similar to the United States and Canada. Why have we failed to build lasting political parties? This is a big question. Actually, this is a one-million dollar question. The answer is simpler than you think. It is division. Political division based on greed has handicapped the development of good and solid political parties during the last quarter of the 19th century and also during the first half of the 20th century. Just like the United States and Canada, we started our building of political parties very well. The liberal party was the first party to be organized in Haiti.

The party was formed in 1970 by the Haitian intellectual elite. Just like parties formed by intellectuals anywhere else, the party was against the military regime of the time. The Liberal party was for a parliamentary democratic government in the country. A parliamentary democracy is a system of government where the members of parliament have more power than the executive branch. One of the main leader of that party was Boyer Bazelais and his friends. They all wanted a more democratic government for the people of Haiti. For a brief period of time, the party controlled parliament in the 1970s. They managed to have strong influence on the executive branch where several secretaries of states resign on the demand of the Liberal party in parliament. In 1874, the party failed to elect someone as president.

Political fractions in the party in 1876 have been the main cause of the disappearance of the liberal party in Haitian politics. The party was divided between itself. Assassinations of former members of the party and oppositions have made it impossible for the party to continue in Haitian politics. A lot of former members of the liberal party seek exile in the Caribbean and other countries.

The ascension to power of president Lysius Salomon in 1879 was an important event in the history of the National Party. That party was the main opposition against the Liberal party. Its main job was to put an end to the liberal party and they have managed to do so. After the dissolution of the liberal party, the National party of president Lysius Salomon was the main party in the country. President Lysius Salomon himself had realized that once president, he did not need the support of the party any longer. In making decisions, the president did not consult with the party. The country became a one-man show. The Political elite of the National Party believed that the power belongs to the people of Haiti. They believed that they were just representing the people of Haiti.

President Lysius Salomon has consolidated his power and did not see the members of the party as people with power and did not pay attention to them. One thing to remember in the evolution of political party in Haiti is that, ever since the assassination of Jean Jacques Dessalines and onward, we have had military governments. Even though a few military leaders have tried to collaborate with political parties in order to gain power, they have never seen them as important and necessary for the organization of the country. President lysius Salomon had done what military leaders before him had done:

belittle the national party. Political tension in the country had put an end to the National Party, brought the people of Haiti in the American Occupation. That occupation would last 19 years from 1915 to 1934.

Like I mentioned in the first chapters, the intellectual elite was not happy with the American Occupation. Even though national division was the main cause for the American Occupation. In the 1930s the Haitian Patriotic Union or L'Union Patriotique Haitienne was founded. The main goal was to fight the American Occupation. The party was founded by Georges Sylvain. The party was very successful in the legislative elections of the 1930s. In 1934, the communist party of Haiti was founded. The party was founded by Jacques Roumain. Due to American influence and the Anti-communist campaign of the United States in the Caribbean and elsewhere in the continent, the party was outlawed by the Haitian government in 1936.

After the American occupation in 1934, a lot of political parties emerged in the country. Those parties were formed as resistance groups long before the formal end of the American Occupation in 1934. After the occupation, parties such as: Parti Socialiste Populaire, le Parti Populaire Sociale Chretien, and le Mouvement des Ouvriers et Paysans founded by Daniel Fignole have come and go. When president Francois Duvalier Came to power in 1957, he persecuted all the political parties. Even though he was the first secretary of the Mouvements des Ouvriers et Paysans founded by Daniel Fignole. President Francois Duvalier dealt harshly with the Communist party of Haiti.

Other political parties such as: Le Parti Populaire

de Liberation Nationale (PPLN), Le parti de Lentente Populaire(PEP), Parti Unifie Des Democrates Haitiens (PUCH), le Rassemblement Des Democrates Nationaux Progressistes d'Haiti(RDNP) and many others were meeting in exile on the telephone. The leader of the party would be for example in Dominican Republic or the United States and talked to the members of the party and told them what to do to mobilize the party against the dictatorship of Francois Duvalier. These political parties along with the Haitian people with the United States and the international community have been very influential in putting an end to the dictatorship of Francois Duvalier and Jean Claude Duvalier in 1986. The Reagan Administration must also receive some credit in the effort. Some people may not agree with that. I respect their opinion.

A culture of weak political parties

The culture of weak political parties is so strong in Haiti, sometimes, politicians think that all they need is popularity. They think that they do not need political parties to start their profession as a political leader. The people in the country usually vote for someone that they like instead of a politician that has given result. The problem is not the people but the institutions that are not working efficiently. A lot of times, when politicians are trying to get elected, they form a provisory political party. A provisory political party is formed to elect a leader or some leaders. Once the job is done, the party dissolved. A provisory political party is different from a permanent political party. No matter what happens on the political scene, the party remains strong.

The Democratic party of the USA is a good example. Many intellectuals blame the weakness of political parties in Haiti on the political environment that exists. Some people believe that, the governments that existed in the country never take the situation of political parties seriously. While this may be true, there are a lot of greed behind the problem. Some politicians in Haiti see a political party as a personal business for me, my wife and my children. That is why we have so many political parties in the country. The countries such as the Bahamas, Jamaica and United States do not have that confusion of political parties, because political parties in these countries have never been a family business but national institutions.

We cannot blame the Haitian people for the crisis of political parties in the country since it is not their job to organize these institutions. Since they do not have any institution to trust, they start trusting politicians who promise them a better tomorrow that will never come. That is why when a leader dies, the political party dies also because it was not set as an institution that can outlast the life of the leader. That leader's ideology dies when the leader dies because that leader was not smart enough to realize that all he can do is to start the movement but somebody else has to finish it not him. The reason why somebody else have to finish it, is that: political struggles require times and efforts. Things will happen but not as soon as you think they will happen.

Who would have believed that the Democratic Party in the United States would have elected a black man as president of the most powerful country on the planet. We have to understand that during the civil war, the democratic party was in favor of keeping the slaves in slavery. President Andrew Jackson, the first president of the Democratic party had his own slaves and therefore was pro slavery. Yet, in a space of more than 150 years, the party that was pro slaves is now the one electing a black man as president of the land. The reason that was possible is the institutionalization of the Democratic Party in the United States. The leaders of political parties in Haiti have to do the same thing. Their vision must go beyond their lifetime. In order for that to happen, political parties in Haiti just like in the industrialized nations, must be institutionalized.

Political Platforms

In a country where most political parties can be seen as family businesses, political platform is the way to go. In an informal way, political platforms can also be seen as political coalition. Usually, a few political parties formed a platform or coalition in order to gain or maintain power in the country. The platform objective is to take power for a specific period of time. After that period, the platform usually dissolves. Political parties that are strong, usually do not form a platform with other parties. Weaker political parties tend to form a platform in order to have a strong voice in the election or in the government. In the United States for example, political parties such as the Republican Party and the Democratic Party do not form platform or coalitions because these parties are strong enough to survive on their own.

In Canada for example, because of the parliamentary system that exists, political coalitions or platforms are set to form the government. Do not misunderstand me, political parties in Canada are very well organized and strong. Parliamentary democracy requires coalitions or platforms because a political party may not have the 2/3 majority needed a lot of times to form the government. While a few political parties in the country such as Fanmi Lavalas, RDNP (Rassemblement Des Democrates Nationaux et Progressistes) and OPL (Organisation du Peuple en Lutte) are very strong, most of the other parties are very weak. Since they are weak, political platform is the way to go. In Haiti, political parties formed coalitions or platforms based on common interests, ideologies and philosophies.

Let's say that four different political parties believe that the government should create jobs for every citizen in the country. These four political parties can form a coalition based on the philosophy of creating jobs for every citizen in the country. Let's say three different political parties want to amend the constitution. These three political parties might form a coalition on the basis of trying to amend the constitution by controlling the government. In Haitian politics, political platforms sometimes are formed between different political parties and other groups because these parties and groups are against a particular leader. The 184 group was formed in Haiti by Andre Apaid, a famous Haitian businessman. Different political parties and other groups in the country were part of the 184 group.

The group was against the social politics of President Jean Bertrand Aristide and the Fanmi Lavalas Political Party. The main objective of the 184 group was to put president Jean Bertrand Aristide out of power by any means necessary. Platforms, coalitions and groups usually act on a provisory agenda. That means their activities are temporary. Sometimes, these groups tend to be permanent. The initial agenda may have been temporary, when things turn in their favors, groups turn to be normal political parties or normal coalitions. As you can see, political platforms, groups or coalitions for the most part are good. In a country as divided as Haiti, one way to maintain political stability is by having platforms, coalitions or groups that are fighting to help the people.

Political parties and political primaries in the 21st century Haiti

Some of the most respected political parties in Haiti today have their root in the fight against the Duvalier Dictatorship. For the political parties that go back to the Duvalier dictatorship, one of their main goals has been accomplished. That goal was to put an end to the Duvalier dictatorship. That happened in 1986. After the Duvalier dictatorship, the parties have failed to organized themselves as political parties do in industrialized nations such as the United States. At the post-Duvalier period, the leader of the party was more influential in politics than the party. Usually a party has a central or a national committee. That was not the case in most Haitian parties.

As far as I can remember, OPL or organization of the people in struggle is the only party in Haiti that I know, the founding leader is dead but the party is still strong. There may be others but I am not aware of them. Even though the military government started at the assassination of Jean Janques Dessalines has a lot to do with the current situation of the country, the lack of organization from the political parties play also a big role in the current predicament. Based on my research, I have to say that, it will be very difficult if not impossible to organize the government in Haiti without the political parties. As dysfunctional as they are, we cannot ignore or overlook them. The government has to deal with them and give them the respect that they deserve.

The names have changed but the most important political parties that we have today in Haiti are rooted in these following parties:

------Le **Comite National du Congres des Mouvements Democratiques** (KonaKom). One of the main objective of that party was to build a better Haiti after the Duvalier dictatorship. It was founded in 1987. Its leader at the time was professor Victor Benoit. Before the election of 1990, KONAKOM became the FNCD or Front National Pour le Changement et la Democratie. FNCD was very instrumental in electing Jean Bertrand Aristide as president in 1990. Father Jean Bertrand Aristide was very influential among the poor people with his theology of liberation. Choosing Jean Bertrand Aristide as the representant of FNCD in the

1990 election, was a last minute choice by the leadership of the party.

-----**Le Mouvement Pour l'instauration de la Democratie en Haiti** (MIDH) was founded in 1986 by the famous Haitian economist Marc L Bazin. Marc L. Bazin became the prime minister in Haiti in 1992. He was very respected for his ideas about government and social issues in the country. He died shortly after the earthquake of January 12, 2010. He did not die in the earthquake.

------**Le Parti Nationaliste Progressiste Revolutionnaire Haitien** was founded by Serge Gilles. Serge Gilles was elected senator in the 1990 election. PANPRA was a member of Socialist International. The main philosophy of PANPRA was the organization of the country to benefit all Haitian in all classes. The party was also founded in 1986.

.......**Le Rassemblement Des Democrates Nationaux Progressistes** (RDNP)was founded in 1981 by professor Leslie Francois Manigat in Caracas, Venezuela. Professor Manigat was very famous for his knowledge in political science in Europe, North America, Venezuela and the Caribbean. Professor Manigat became president in 1988 for a brief period of time. Today, his Wife Mirlande Manigat is the leader of the party.

........**Organisation du Peuple en luttre (OPL)** was founded after the division in the organization of people's in struggle in the mid-1990s after the return of Jean Bertrand Aristide as president in 1994. Today, Organisation du Peuple en Lutte is one of the most important political party in the nation. OPL has survived the death of his main important leader, Gerard Pierre Charles. The political tradition in

Haiti is simple. Whenever a leader dies, the party dies. OPL has proven they can go beyond the life of Gerard Pierre Charles. That proves, Gerard Pierre Charles and leaders such as Dr. Sauveur Pierre Etienne have done a great job in institutionalizing the party.

------**Fanmi Lavalas (FL)** is one of the most popular party in the country. Fanmi Lavalas was created in the Mid-1990s after a split in the organization politique Lavalas or OPL. The party founder president Jean Bertrand Aristide returned to Haiti in March 2011 and ever since is the one leading the party. The party has a secretary but Aristide is the head man in charge. If the government is stable and well organized, all these parties including Fanmi Lavalas can make a great difference in creating peace and prosperity for all Haitians.

A political primary every five years

If political parties or coalitions are going to survive in Haiti, the leadership has to think differently. They have to stop seeing themselves as God. Only God is eternal. All of us are mortal. God does not operate in time, we do. Therefore, the only hope is to create institutions that will outlast a politician lifetime. There is a national council of political parties in Haiti and I think that is a good thing. That council must force all the political parties in the country to elect a new leader every five years.

Now here is the interesting part. Since the political parties in Haiti are not that big, the leadership of the party will have to choose who is going to represent the party in the elections and who is not going to represent the party. I propose a political primary every five years in the country. All the political parties or coalitions will be allowed to participate in that primary. The Haitian people are not going to vote for the leaders of the party or coalitions but for the names only. The real election would happen after the primary. The five political parties or coalitions that have the most vote, will be allowed to participate in the elections all over the country for a period of five years.

The political primary every five years is just an idea. Do not forget that, this book proposes a parliamentary system of government for the country. If that happens, the crisis of political parties will not have a major effect in destabilizing the country since the government will come from parliament where some of the most popular political parties will be represented. The president will play a ceremonial role such as the case in Italy, Trinidad, Germany and the governor general of Canada. In this system, political parties do not have the power to destabilize the country because you do not have the situation of one party in power vs another party out of power. With a parliamentary system of government, you do not really need political primary every five years because this regime solves this problem automatically.

CHAPTER 7

A FEW OF THE WORLD MOST ORGANIZED POLITICAL PARTIES

OPL (People's in Struggle Organization, Haiti)

OPL is one of the most organized political parties in Haiti. I think, it is the only organized political party in the country. When talking about the most well organized political parties in the world, OPL is the only one that can represent Haiti according to my knowledge. Its beginning goes back, however, to the development of a vision, of a political thought which has its source in the Continental Conference of Solidarity with Haiti or the Conference of Panama. Gérard Pierre-Charles, influential member of the Unified Party of Haitian Communists (PUCH) is the promoter of the Haitian Democratic Committee of Mexico, an organization bringing together various political tendencies. He was one of the organizers in 1981 of this great international demonstration against the Duvalier dictatorship which marks the partnership towards a joint work in the making of the various currents of the opposition, in particular the Marxists and the Christians.

Back from his 26-year exile in Haiti, he plans to continue the fight according to a vision of militancy better suited to the reality of the country and the world. He distances himself from the PUCH. He begins to build a network comprising activists coming from various horizons of political thought and action, in particular of liberation theology, grassroots groups, peasant movements. From this dynamic will be born, in the movement of the fight for democratic freedoms from 1986 to 1990 and especially of the fight against the military coup of 1991, the OPL (Lavalas Political Organization later become Organization of the People in Struggle) whose he was the General Coordinator until his death on October 10, 2004.

Founded on December 5 and 6, 1991 on the occasion of the Extraordinary Assembly bringing together in clandestinity eighty-two delegates from all the departments of the country and from the diaspora fighting against the military coup and for the return to constitutional order, the OPL undergoes three distinct stages in its historical development.

The first stage known as of formation, consolidation and affirmation of the Party goes from 1991 to the holding of the 2nd National Congress in December 2004. During this period, the OPL manifests its commitment to social and political change in Haiti, in particular by being at the forefront of all the fights against authoritarian and dictatorial tendencies, the anarchic and antidemocratic drifts of the powers in place. It is the resistance organization par excellence, strong in the activism of its members, the courage and rectitude of its leaders. It lays the foundations for a national, permanent institution, forging an image of a fighting organization, serious and responsible in its positions.

At the 2nd National Congress held on December 17, 18, 19, 2004, the OPL adopted a new political line. It intends to model its structures, strengthen its institutional capacities, transform itself into an instrument of conquest and management of state power, in addition to being a resistance organization. It lobbies for the holding of elections, participates in them at all levels, and ranks among the main political parties both through its representation in Parliament and in local authorities, the discipline of its elected representatives, the strength of its proposals and through the quality of its activists, the organization and extent of its structures on the national territory.

During this second stage of its development initiated by the 2nd National Congress, the OPL participates in the effort to socialize political forces. It contributes to the development and adoption of the "Pact for Stability and Governance" to which several political parties adhere before the 2005 elections. In the line of thought and action contained in this pact, it founded with other parties the Convention of Haitian Political Parties, a space for dialogue and conviviality between actors of different political orientations and ideologies, which define as a permanent forum for debates on issues of national interest, the promotion and defense of political parties and the normalization of political life. The OPL is meant to be and truly is, at this period of its development, an institution. It ceases to be the property of its members to become a national heritage. It thus approaches the third stage of its history which begins at the 4th National Congress of the

Party, held in Les Cayes, in the South department, on August 26, 27, 28, 2011.

The Democratic Party (USA)

The Democratic Party is one of the two major political parties in the United States, along with its main rival, the Republican Party. The heritage goes back to Thomas Jefferson and James Madison's Democratic-Republican Party. The modern-day Democratic Party was founded around 1828 by supporters of Andrew Jackson, making it the world's oldest active political party.

In its early years, the Party supported limited government, state sovereignty, and slavery, while opposing banks. Since Franklin D. Roosevelt and his New Deal coalition in the 1930s, the Democratic Party has promoted a social liberal platform. Well into the 20th century, the party had conservative pro-business and Southern conservative-populist wings; following the New Deal, however, the conservative wing of the party largely withered outside the South. The New Deal coalition of 1932–1964 attracted strong support from voters of recent European extraction—many of whom were Catholics based in the cities. After the Civil Rights Act of 1964 and the Voting Rights Act of 1965, the core bases of the two parties shifted, with the Southern states becoming more reliably Republican in presidential politics and the Northeastern states becoming more reliably Democratic.

The once-powerful labor union element became smaller after the 1970s, although the working class remains an important component of the Democratic base. People living in urban areas, women, college graduates, and millennials, as well as sexual, religious, and racial minorities, also tend to support the Democratic Party.

The Democratic Party's philosophy of modern liberalism advocates social and economic equality, along with the welfare state. It seeks to provide government regulation in the economy to promote the public interest. Environmental protection, support for organized labor, maintenance and expansion of social programs, affordable college tuition, universal health care, equal opportunity, and consumer protection form the core of the party's economic policy. On social issues, it advocates campaign finance reform, LGBT rights, criminal justice and immigration reform, stricter gun laws, and the legalization of marijuana.

Fifteen Democrats have served as President of the United States. The first was Andrew Jackson, who was the seventh president and served from 1829 to 1837. The most recent was Barack Obama, who was the 44th and held office from 2009 to 2017. As of 2020, the Democrats hold a majority in the House of Representatives, 15 state governors (governorship and both legislative chambers), the mayoralty of most major American cities and 19 total state legislatures. Four of the nine sitting justices of the Supreme Court were appointed by Democratic presidents.

The Liberal Party of Canada

The Liberal Party of Canada or le Parti libéral du Canada is the longest-serving and oldest active federal political party in Canada. The party has dominated federal politics for much of Canada's history. The Liberals held power for almost 70 years in the 20th century, which is more than any other party in a developed country. As a result, it has sometimes been referred to as Canada's "natural governing party".

The party believes in the principles of liberalism, and generally sits at the centre to centre-left of the Canadian political system, with the Conservative Party positioned to the centre-right to the right and the New Democratic Party (who at times aligned itself with the Liberals during minority governments), occupying the centre-left to left. Like their federal Conservative Party rivals, the party is often described as a "big tent", attracting support from a broad spectrum of voters. In the late 1970s, Prime Minister Pierre Elliott Trudeau stated that his Liberal Party adhered to the "radical centre".

The Liberals' signature policies and legislative decisions include universal health care, the Canada Pension Plan, Canada Student Loans, peacekeeping, multilateralism, official bilingualism, official multiculturalism, patriating the Canadian constitution and the entrenchment of Canada's Charter of Rights and Freedoms, the Clarity Act, legalizing same-sex marriage, euthanasia, and cannabis, national carbon pricing, and reproductive choice.

In the 2015 federal election, the Liberal Party under Justin Trudeau had its best result since the 2000 election, winning 39.5 percent of the popular vote and 184 seats, gaining a majority of seats in the House of Commons. In the 2019 federal election, they lost their majority, winning 157 seats, but they still remained the largest party in the House.

The Socialist Party (France)

The Socialist Party is a social-democratic political party in France. The PS was for decades the largest party of the French centre-left and used to be one of the two major political parties in the French Fifth Republic, along with The Republicans. It replaced the earlier French Section of the Workers' International in 1969. The PS is a member of the Party of European Socialists, Progressive Alliance and Socialist International.

The PS first won power in 1981, when its candidate François Mitterrand was elected President of France in the 1981 presidential election. Under Mitterrand, the party achieved a governing majority in the National Assembly from 1981 to 1986 and again from 1988 to 1993. PS leader Lionel Jospin lost his bid to succeed Mitterrand as president in the 1995 presidential election against Rally for the Republic leader Jacques Chirac, but he became Prime Minister in a cohabitation government after the 1997 legislative election, a position Jospin held until 2002, when he was again defeated in the 2002 presidential election.

Ségolène Royal, the party's candidate for 2007 presidential election, was defeated by conservative UMP candidate Nicolas Sarkozy. The PS won most of regional and local elections and for the first time in more than fifty years, it won control of the Senate in the 2011 Senate election. On May 6, 2012, François Hollande, the First Secretary of the party from 1997 to 2008, was elected President and the next month the party won a majority in the 2012 legislative election. During his term, Hollande battled with high unemployment, poor opinion ratings and a splinter group of left-wing Socialist MPs known as frondeurs (rebels).

On December 1, 2016, Francois Hollande declined to seek re-election and the PS subsequently organized a presidential primary. Left-wing Benoit Hamon was designated as the Socialist candidate after defeating former Prime Minister Manuel Valls. Facing the emergence of centrist Emmanuel Macron and left-winger Jean-Luc Mélenchon, Hamon failed to re-establish the PS leadership on the centre-left and finished 5th in the 2017 presidential election, gathering only 6.36 percent of the votes. The party then lost the majority of its MPs in the 2017 legislative election, securing 26 seats and becoming the fourth-biggest group in the National Assembly.

The PS also formed several figures who acted at the international level and were from the party, including Jacques Delors, who was the eighth President of the European Commission from 1985 to 1994 and the first person to serve three terms in that office; Dominique Strauss-kahn, who was the Managing Director of the International Monetary Fund from 2007 to 2011; and Pascal Lamy, who was Director-General of the World Trade Organization from 2005 to 2013.

The African National Congress (South Africa)

The African National Congress (ANC) is the Republic of South Africa's governing political party. It has been the ruling party of post-apartheid South Africa since the election of Nelson Mandela in the 1994 election, winning every election since then.

Founded on January 8, 1912 by John Langalibalele Dube

in Bloemfontein as the South African Native National Congress (SANNC), its primary mission was to bring all Africans together as one people, to defend their rights and freedoms. This included giving full voting rights to black South Africans and mixed-race South Africans and, from 1948 onwards, to end the system of apartheid introduced by the Nationalist Party government after their election in that year.

The ANC originally attempted to use non-violent protests to end apartheid; however, the Sharpeville massacre in March 1960, in which 69 black Africans were shot and killed by police and hundreds wounded during a peaceful protest, contributed to deteriorating relations with the South African government. On April 8, 1960, the administration of Charles Robberts Swart banned the ANC in South Africa After the ban, the ANC formed the Umkhonto we Sizwe (Spear of the Nation) to fight against apartheid utilising guerrilla warfare and sabotage.

After 30 years of exiled struggle, during which many ANC members had been imprisoned or forced abroad, the country began its move towards full democracy. On February 3, 1990, State President F. W. de Klerk lifted the ban on the ANC and released Nelson Mandela from prison on February 11, 1990. On March 17, 1992, the apartheid referendum was passed by the white only electorate, removing apartheid and allowing the ANC to run in the 1994 election, which for the first time allowed all South Africans to vote for their national government. Since the 1994 election, the ANC has performed better than 55% in all general elections.

All Progressives Congress (Nigeria)

Formed in February 2013, the party is the result of a merger of Nigeria's three biggest opposition parties – the Action Congress of Nigeria (ACN), the Congress for Progressive Change (CPC), the All Nigeria Peoples Party (ANPP), a faction of the All Progressives Grand Alliance (APGA) and the new PDP - a fraction of the ruling **SUB** People's Democratic Party.

The party received approval from the nation's Independent National Electoral Commission (INEC) on July 31, 2013 to become a political party and subsequently withdrew the operating licenses of the three parties that merged (the ACN, CPC and ANPP). In March 2013, it was reported that two other associations – African People's Congress and All Patriotic Citizens – also applied for INEC registration, adopting APC as an acronym as well, reportedly "a development interpreted to be a move to thwart the successful coalition of the opposition parties, ahead of the 2015 general elections." It was reported in April 2013 that the party was considering changing their name to the All Progressive Congress of Nigeria (APCN) to avoid further complications.

In November 2013, five serving Governors from the governing PDP defected to the APC, as well as 49 legislators who joined the ranks of 137 legislators in the APC as a result of the prior merger of the smaller opposition parties. This initially gave the APC a slim majority of 186 legislators in the Lower House out of a total of 360 legislators; however, subsequent political wrangling and pressure from political factions and interests outside the National Assembly of Nigeria, gave the party only 37 additional legislators, thus giving the APC a nominal majority of 172 out of 360 Legislators, as opposed to the PDP's 171 (though some smaller PDP-allied parties hold the balance of the other seats). This was further confirmed when the party seated 179 members on January 15, 2015 when the House resumed after a long recess to finally affirm its majority.

The labour party (United Kingdom)

The Labour Party is a centre-left political party in the United Kingdom that has been described as an alliance of social democrats, democratic socialists and trade unionists. In all general elections since 1922, Labour has been either the governing party or the Official Opposition. There have been six Labour Prime Ministers and eight ministries.

The Labour Party was founded in 1900, having grown out of the trade union movement and socialist parties of the 19th century. It overtook the Liberal Party to become the main opposition to the Conservative Party in the early 1920s, forming two minority governments under Ramsay MacDonald in the 1920s and early 1930s. Labour served in the wartime coalition of 1940–1945, after which Clement Attlee's Labour government established the National Health Service and expanded the welfare state from 1945 to 1951. Under Harold Wilson and James Callaghan, Labour again governed from 1964 to 1970 and 1974 to 1979. In the 1990s, Tony Blair took Labour to the centre as part of his New

Labour project which governed the UK under Blair and then Gordon Brown from 1997 to 2010.

Labour is a member of the Party of European Socialists and Progressive Alliance, and holds observer status in the Socialist International.

The Christian Democratic Union (Germany)

The Christian Democratic Union of Germany is a Christian democratic and liberal conservative political party in Germany. The party was founded in 1945 as an interdenominational Christian party, the CDU effectively succeeded the pre-war Catholic Centre Party, with many former members joining the party, including its first leader Konrad Adenauer. The party also included politicians of other backgrounds, including liberals and conservatives. As a result, the party claims to represent "Christian-social, liberal and conservative" elements. The CDU is generally pro-European in outlook. Black is the party's customary colour. Other colours include red for the logo, orange for the flag, and black-red-gold for the corporate design.

The CDU has headed the federal government since 2005 under Angela Merkel, who also served as the party's leader from 2000 until 2018. The CDU previously led the federal government from 1949 to 1969 and 1982 to 1998. Germany's three longest-serving post-war Chancellors have all come from the CDU; Helmut Kohl (1982–1998), Angela Merkel (2005–present), and Konrad Adenauer (1949–1963). The party also leads the governments of six of Germany's sixteen states.

The CDU is a member of the Centrist Democrat International, the International Democrat Union and the European People's Party (EPP).

Workers' Party (Brazil)

Brazil is one of the largest country in the world in term of population, economy and size. The worker's party is one of the largest political party in Latin America and one of the most successful in Brazil in term of election results. The party was founded in 1980. The Workers party governed at the federal level in a coalition government with several other parties from January 1, 2003 to August 31, 2016. After the 2002 parliamentary election, PT became the largest party in the Chamber of Deputies and the largest in the Federal Senate for the first time. With the highest approval rating in the history of the country, former President Luiz Inácio Lula da Silva is PT's most prominent member.

The Communist Party of China

Just like Brazil, China is one of the largest country in the world in term of Population, Economy and geographic size. The Chinese Communist Party or the Communist Party of China (CPC), is the founding and ruling political party of the People's Republic of China (PRC) and the second largest political party in the world after India's Bharatiya Janata Party. The CCP is the only governing party within mainland China, it permits only eight other, subordinated parties to co-exist, those making up the United Front. It was founded in 1921, chiefly by Chen Duxiu and Li Dazhao. The party grew quickly, and by 1949 it had driven the Kuomintang (KMT)'s Nationalist Government from mainland China to Taiwan after the Chinese Civil War, leading to the establishment of the People's Republic of China on October 1, 1949. It also controls the country's armed forces, the People's Liberation Army (PLA).

When it comes to its organization, The CCP is organised on the basis of democratic centralism, a principle conceived by Russian Marxist theoretician Vladimir Lenin which entails democratic and open discussion on policy on the condition of unity in upholding the agreed upon policies. Theoretically, the highest body of the CCP is the National Congress, convened every fifth year. When the National Congress is not in session, the Central Committee is the highest body, but since the body meets normally only once a year most duties and responsibilities are in the hands of the Politburo and its Standing Committee

The Liberal Democratic Party of Japan

Most Haitians love Japan for Technology and Cars. Political parties in Japan have been well organized and well established. We can learn a lot from them when it comes to the organization of political parties. Japan has been a peaceful and a stable country since world war 2. The LDP has almost continuously been in power since its foundation in 1955—a period called the 1955 System—with the exception of a period between 1993 and 1994, and again from 2009 to 2012. In the

2012 election, it regained control of the government. It holds 285 seats in the lower house and 113 seats in the upper house, and in coalition with the Komeito, the governing coalition has a supermajority in both houses as of 2020.

Spanish Socialist Workers Party

The most successful and important political party in Spain is the Spanish Socialist Workers' Party, founded in 1879 and currently (in 2021) with more than 150,000 members. The party supports free health care for all, better working conditions for workers, women's rights, gay rights, better wages for workers and many other socialist programs. One of its affiliations is with the organization of the Socialist International. Spain has a system of parliamentary government where the people of the country choose the members of parliament (senators and deputies). Members of parliament, mainly the chamber of deputies, choose the prime minister from the largest party or coalition in parliament for a period of 4 years. The Head of State is the King. The country has a well organized judicial system.

CHAPTER 8

THE PERMANENT ELECTORAL COUNCIL

The CEP and the Military governments

I have already made it clear that, a military dictatorship was installed in Haiti since the death of Jean Jacques Dessalines in 1806 to the military Coup of September 30, 1991. That military was one of the main reason why the CEP was not that successful in making democratic elections in the country. Leaders such as: Toussaint, Dessalines, Petion, Christophe had constitutions where they were president or king for life. That means the institutions of the country were not democratic. If there was an election, it was not an election but a selection where the most powerful person put his friends or family members in the government. There have been a few exceptions to that rule however.

The election between Francois Duvalier, Louis Dejoie and Daniel Fignole in 1957 has been described by some people as a democratic election since Daniel Fignole fled the country into exile and did not participate in the process. A lot of historians believe that he would have beaten Francois

Duvalier if he did not go into exile. Others believe that the election was not democratic since Daniel Fignole did not participate but was forced to flee the country. Another case is the general election of January 17, 1988 organized by the CEP. Some believe that power was given to president Francois Manigat by the military machine under Henri Namphy. Others believe that the election was democratic. We will never know for certain what happened. One thing was clear in that election: The voters did not turnout.

Less than 10% of eligible people voted in that election. You might ask yourself why the voter turnout was so low. The reason was simple. The people did not believe the system was democratic and did not want to go risking their lives to elect people that they did not feel were going to change their predicament.

The CEP and the 1990 election

When President Jean Claude Duvalier left Haiti for France in 1986, he left behind a CNG or national council of government or Conseil National de Gouvernement. That council was made up of Williams Regala, Max Valles, Prosper Avril, Gerard Gourgue and Alix Cineas. After President Prosper Avril was ousted from power, general Herard Abraham became president for three days and passed power to Ertha Pascal Trouillot who was the supreme court judge. It was a democratic process because it follows the constitution of 1987. According to many, Ertha Pascal Trouillot would organize the first democratic election in the history of Haiti. That election in 1990 brought Jean Bertrand Aristide a former priest and an advocate for the poor to power. Jean Bertrand Aristide, Louis Dejoe and Marc L Bazin received the most votes during that election.

Le Front National pour le Changement et la Democratie (FNCD) was more a platform than a party. It came from an alliance between KONAkOM or le Comite National du Congres des Mouvements Democratiques and PNDPH or L'Alliance Nationale pour la Democratie et le Progres. FNCD was very popular in the 1990s because it came from two major anti-Duvalier political parties. FNCD chose Aristide at the last minute to represent the party in the 1990 election. Some people believe that it was not a wise idea to choose someone outside of the party as leader. Some believe that it was a nice choice because father Aristide was very popular at that moment. No-one will know exactly what happened between Aristide and FNCD after the election of November 1990.

It was clear that the major members of FNCD were not part of the government. Rene Garcia Preval became prime minister instead of Victor Benoit or Evans Paul. Some believe that Aristide betrays FNCD, others believe that FNCD betrays Aristide. We will never know what happened for sure to create division between Aristide and the leadership of FNCD. Like I said before, it was clear that FNCD was not part of the government. By political protocol, Aristide should have chosen some people from FNCD to be part of the government. He did not do that. Maybe FNCD had made a mistake in choosing someone they did not know in a personal way. The September 30, 1991 complicated the political discussion in a big way because president Jean

Bertran Aristide was sent to exile. The bigger problem here is not FNCD or president Aristide. The bigger problem here is the semi-presidential system of government set by the 1987 constitution.

Just like in a presidential system of government, the semi-presidential system of government can be a one- man show. Once people take power, their personality can change in a minute. In a semi-presidential system of government, the power is in the hand of one person. In a parliamentary system, it is different. The power is shared between different parties in Parliament. If Haiti had a parliamentary system, FNCD could have chosen Aristide and still be in charge of the country. They would choose Aristide to represent just one city not the whole country. In a parliamentary system, the party or platform or coaltion represent the country not just one person and that is a big difference.

The CEP and the 2006 election

The CEP set up by Gerard Latortue's Administration had for goal to have a democratic election in Haiti. Gerard Latortue promised free and fair election in the entire country. When he first came to power after the departure of president Jean Bertrand Aristide in 2004, he promised a government of coalition. Forming a government of coalition was very difficult if not impossible for Latortue because of the weakness of the system in Haiti. Gerard Latortue who was foreign minister under President Leslie Francois Manigat in 1988 and a United Nations official thought that things were going to be easy. That was not the case.

Gerard Latortue was organizing an election that the people of Haiti was waiting for to return Aristide to Haiti. In the people's mind, the best way to do that is to elect the person they believe was the closest to Aristide. Here I am talking about longtime friend of Aristide, Rene Garcia Preval. When I was in Haiti in the early 1990s, people used to say Titid et Ti rene. People in Haiti believed that Aristide and Preval were twins. In a country with an unorganized system of government, politics can easily divide people. Some people think that only happens in Haiti. The same thing is going on right now in the United States. It is happening in the United States at a lower level. The more you understand a semi-presidential system of government, the more you realized that the system in itself create division. It is a one -man show.

The president seems to have more power than parliament. You can bring in the government your friends and family members. In a Parliamentary System it is the opposite. That is why the CEP in the 2006 election had a hard time organizing the election. Prime Minister Gerard Latortue had the power to shift the election to the right or to the left. The people in Haiti were not ready to accept someone they did not vote for as president. The international community did not want to find itself in a desperate situation that they could not control. Prime Minister Gerard Latortue had to use common sense and logic and that was exactly what he did.

The Election was delayed 4 times because of the political instability that followed after the removal of Aristide as president in 2004. The election finally took place on February 7, 2006. It was a difficult job for the CEP to do because it was largely controlled by a government that wanted things in its favor. That was not uncommon because previous governments had done the exact same thing. In the first round of the election, President Preval was leading in the poll with more than 48% of the vote. It was later on discovered that there was fraud to prevent Preval from becoming president for a second term of five years. After recounts and recounts of votes, President Preval had about 51.1% of the vote and he was declared the winner of the election.

Not only President Preval won the election, his political party Lespwa won a majority in parliament. Politicians such as Leslie Francois Manigat, Charles Henri Baker, Marc L Bazin among others participated without great success. Late catholic priest father Gerard Jean Juste and wealthy Haitian businessman from Texas Dumarsais Simeus were not allowed to participate in that election. Father Jean Juste was put in jail. He later died in Miami. The supporters of Fanmi Lavalas were very furious because Fanmi Lavalas was not allowed to participate in the election and because father Jean Juste was put in Jail without goood reason. At the end of the day, they had president Preval. After president Preval was inaugurated as president, he turned out to be not the politician that the people of Haiti was expected him to be and that was a big disappointment for the people of Haiti who sacrificed so much to get him elected as president.

The CEP and the 2010-2011 election

Just like in 2006, the CEP had a great job to do in the 2010-2011 presidential and parliamentary elections. President Preval was in power. He was a great disappointment for the people of Haiti. They did not want to have anything to do with him and they did not want someone close to him to be president of the country. The job became more and more difficult for the CEP because president Preval wanted someone close to him to be president while the people wanted someone that they can relate to. The January 12, 2010 earthquake had a large impact on the election. The situation forced the government to postpone things. Wyclef Jean was excluded from the election because of residence issues.

Fanmi Lavalas was also excluded because the critics believed that Jean Bertrand Aristide was not present in the country and he was not able to sign the list of the people that should represent the party in the election. Some people believed that there should not be any election in the country because of the aftermath of the earthquake. Others believed that there should be election all over the country. The pro-election groups such as the United States, the United Nations, Canada and France put enough pressure on President Preval to have the election. The people of Haiti also wanted the election because they did not want to see president Preval remained president of the country.

Basically the first round of the election was about then-musician Michel Joseph Martelly, Professor Mirlande Manigat, engineer Jude Celestin and the other candidates. People who understand Haitian politics understand the outcome before it is proclaimed by the CEP. For the Haitian people to vote for you, there are two requirements: the first is to be popular and loved by them and the second is to have the support of someone popular that they like. If you meet one of those two requirements, you do not have any problem in winning elections. Candidates such as Charles Henri Baker, Yvon Neptune, Jacques Edouard Alexis are very qualified to lead but they are not that popular among the people. After the first round of the election, it was clear to the CEP, the Haitian people and the international community that Michel Joseph Martelly, Mirlande Manigat and Jude Celestin had the highest percentage of vote.

In the second round Musician Michel Joseph Martelly was declared the winner by the CEP. It was not an easy job to do because Mirlande Manigat and Jude Celestin were establishment candidates. Michel Martelly was an outsider. Even though he was an outsider he was well loved and well known by the Haitian people. Even though Mirlande Manigat has been in politics for decades, the result of the election proved that the people of Haiti understood the message and the political campaign of Michel Joseph Martelly better than they understood her message and her political campaign. In spites of the criticisms, if the right institutions exist, the CEP has proven again and again that democratic elections can take place in Haiti. The 1990 election, the 1995 election, the 2006 election and the 2010-2011 have been all democratic.

At the beginning of all these elections there have been all kind of problems and all kind of issues, but at the end, the people of Haiti had what they want. The 1995 election was one of the most peaceful compared to others. President Aristide returned to power in 1994 but was unable to continue his term beyond five years. He passed the presidency democratically to the then-prime minister Rene Garcia Preval who was very respected and very popular at the time. Just like countries such as Jamaica and the Bahamas, when the intellectual elite manages to give the Haitian people a parliamentary system of government, Haiti will be one of the most peaceful country in the Caribbean and the world.

The CEP under president Joseph Michel Martelly

There is a political dispute as I am writing this book concerning the permanent electoral council. Due to political instability, Haiti usually has a temporary or provisory electoral council not permanent. President Michel Joseph Martelly wanted a permanent electoral council. Based on the amended version of the 1987 constitution, the 9 members of the permanent electoral council should be set on the basis of 3 from the president or the executive branch, 3 from the supreme court of the country and 3 from the parliament. The three members of parliament must have the support of 2/3 of the senate and the chamber of deputies.

The Executive branch and the Supreme Court have been able to choose their members but the parliament has yet to do so. The reason for that is the fact that the senate is not complete. 1/3 of its members must be re-elected. The members of the legislature believe that, if they choose their 3 members with the current condition in the country, they would violate the constitution. It is a very complex problem. Logically speaking, it will be very difficult for the members of parliament to choose their representants in the future permanent electoral council with that 2/3 majority of both chambers. The constitution or the amended constitution made it difficult to have simple and efficient elections in the country. The permanent electoral council has been a source of tension in Haitian politics. The primary reason for that was the army. The army set a military government that made it impossible for the country to have a democratic government.

With the army gone, the main reason for the crisis in the permanent electoral council is the way it is set in the constitution along with unorganized political parties and the semi presidential system.

Just like I have mentioned before, we are in a constitutional period in the history of Haiti. We need to amend the constitution to create a parliamentary system of government in the country. A parliamentary regime is the only system that I know that can create the political stability and economic prosperity that the people of Haiti want. In the chapter concerning the political parties, I believe we must have a political primary every five years to choose the parties or coalitions that can lead the country the best for a period of five years. The CEP should come from these five political parties or coalitions. Organizing the CEP from the three branches of government and live the political parties behind will not solve our problem.

The organization of the CEP should come first from the political parties that win the primary to a list submitted to the senate and finally from a list submitted to the president by the senate. I propose a ten-members CEP. Two persons from each of the five political parties or coalition that win the primary before the general election. The solution of the problem is simpler than we believe. In spite of that fragile semi-presidential system, we have had democratic elections. I believe Haiti can do better with better institutions. The beauty of the parliamentary government is that: There is no direct presidential election to create crisis among the political parties and the CEP. Nobody is directly elected to any ministerial post but a departemental seat or parliamentary seat or communal seat. This system of government in itself solve at least 3/4 of the political problems of the country.

The CEP and the 30% quota for political integration of women

From the presidential election of 1990, where a female president organized one of the most successful elections in the history of Haitian politics to the presidency of Joseph Michel Martelly in 2011 where more women were integrated into politics, the debate for more integration and participation of women in Haitian politics is with us. The fact that we are talking about it, is a starting point. Culturally speaking, Haitian society considers politics as a profession of men. This means that, unless we come up with strong laws to defend women's participation, it will never happen on a large scale. Article 17-1 of the amended 1987 constitution which requires the 30% quota is an excellent starting point.

Countries like the United States, Canada, France, Germany and many others have made great progress and we can use them as examples. Prime Minister Justin Trudeau's Office in 2015 was made up of 50% men and 50% women. One of the main reasons for this is that Canada has a system of parliamentary government that facilitates the integration of women. At the departmental level, the French have come up with binomial elections where two people (a man and a woman) must be elected in each constituency, which gives women a 50% chance of political integration. I do not support this binomial system for Haiti for cultural reasons. Germany Chancellor is female (Angela Merkel), U.S. Vice President Kamala Harris is female, current presidents of Trinidad and Tobago and Ethiopia are females (2021)

Based on information made public by Alter Press which is a Haitian journalistic organization, the Martelly / Lamothe administration is the only administration in the history of Haitian politics to respect the 30% quota in 2012. Although I do not defend here binomial elections such as the case in France for Haiti, the only way to solve the problem is to attack it at the root. This means that the permanent electoral council or the provisional electoral council must respect the quota itself, the CEP has to force all political parties to respect it, through the government, the CEP must force the private sector organizations, private companies, all government institutions to respect it.

A parliamentary system of government, direct elections for municipal councils, departmental councils among others are an excellent way to improve the electoral participation of women, maintain or increase the quota of 30% and reduce these cultural prejudices that have destroyed the haitian society for decades.

Types of elections, voting system and the French model

To end this chapter on the electoral system in Haiti, dividing the electoral calendar into different types of elections will make things easier and create a climate of political stability and public security. In the United States, the electoral calendar is very confusing and difficult to understand. The French model where the electoral calendar is divided into four main parts (municipal elections, departmental / regional elections, election to the national assembly and presidential elections) is a good example for us in Haiti. These four elections took place on four separate dates. These elections take place every five and six years in France. We can have in Haiti, elections for communal sections / municipal, departmental elections, legislative elections and presidential elections every five years on separate dates.

There are three main types of voting systems and all of them have been applied in France: **first past the post** voting when electors vote for one candidate, **binomial voting** when electors vote for two candidate at the same time and **Party list voting** when the electors vote for more than two candidates at the same time. I propose the first past the post voting system for Haiti since it is easier to understand and to apply. Canada, France at the national assembly level and the United Kingdom have used this system very well.

Unlike France where the people directly choose the president, the parliament will choose the president in Haiti just like in Italy, Trinidad and Tobago, Germany, etc. to avoid the confusion and chaos that accompany the French direct presidential election in countries without deep democratic traditions such as countries in Latin America and Africa.

CHAPTER 9

THE PARLIAMENT AND THE CANADIAN MODEL

The Canadian parliament is made up of 443 members at least for the year 2020. 338 members for the House of Commons who serve five years and 105 members for the senate. The parliament is bicameral or two chambers. The senators represent different districts that are larger than the districts of the House of Commons. Senators in Canada just like in France are appointed not elected. They also serve for life until retirement age. The process of appointing senators and appointing them for life will not work in Haiti but everything else will work if we learn from this great model of parliament.

Another great model besides the Canadian model is the Italian model of parliament. Since 1946 when the monarchy was abolished, Italy has had one of the greatest democracies in the world. Their parliament or the legislative branch is one of the most organized and modern in the world. The Italian parliament is a great model for developed and developing countries. The parliament is bicameral meaning two chambers: the chamber of the senate is made up of 315 senators and the chamber of deputies is made up of 630 deputies in 2020. These numbers will be reduce in 2023 general election following the 2020 referendum in Italy. Some of these senators and deputies are chosen. Most of them are elected by people in different constituencies for five years during just one election. With the exception of appointing senators and deputies and appointing them for life, this system is a great example for Haiti and any developing country.

Jean Jacques Dessalines had left behind a military government that had handicapped the most powerful political and public institution in the country, the Parliament. It is not clear when the parliament was set. In the early days of the Republic, the country did not have a parliament but a legal Council that served at the pleasure of the president. The president was elected for life. Whatever he wanted, he gets it from the legal council. That is why the country has had 23 constitutions. Let's take for example: Toussaint, Dessalines and Petion, each man had his own constitution or his own legal council or his own parliament to passed laws that made it easier for him to govern the country. A parliament under military rules will never be strong enough to defend the interest of the people and the nation.

That is why until today there is in Haiti a culture of disrespect from the presidency toward the parliament. The presidential legal council called parliament had created that culture of disrespect toward the parliament. The legal council called parliament of 1801 wrote a constitution that gave Toussaint the power to govern for life and to name his own successor. It was the same thing with Christophe when he was president in the North and Jean Jacques Dessalines after independence. Each man had a legal council that wrote a constitution for the benefit of the leader in the name of the people. The 1816 parliament voted a constitution that consider only the bills proposed by president Alexandre Petion.

The constitution of 1874 granted President Michel Domingue the power to dissolve parliament and to rule by decree. President Francois Duvalier managed in 1957 to have parliament voted a constitution that gave him unlimited power to do whatever he wanted. In 1964, most of the members of parliament were closely associated with François Duvalier. They passed laws that proclaimed Francois Duvalier president for life. No real parliament will hang itself by giving the president more power than necessary. These parliaments were not truly parliament in the real sense of the word. They were legal councils made by the presidents and the military machine to serve their personal interest.

The 1987 constitution and parliament

When comparing with others, the 1987 constitution is the best constitution that the country has had in the past 200 years of independence. Under that constitution, the parliament has had more power than before. Articles 88 to 132 enumerated the power that parliament has when it comes to its function in the country. It is true that this constitution is better than the other ones, it is far from normal. That is why I believe that the country is still in a constitutional period or constitutional crisis. As long as the country is in this unstable state, parliament will not be able to function correctly. Article 88 started by saying how many chambers the legislature should have. It stated clearly that the parliament of the country is made up of two chambers: the chamber of deputies and the senate. Article 89 deals with the lower chamber of parliament. That is the chamber of deputies.

Article 89 clearly stated that the chamber of deputies should not have less than 70 deputies. Article 91 stated the requirement for someone to be elected a deputy in the country. Requirements such as: 25 years of age, never renounced to the Haitian nationality, not being in jail while trying to run for office among others are stated clearly in the constitution. Articles 94 deals with the senate. The number of the senators should not be more than 30. The constitution stated clearly that 3 senators per department should be elected in the country. Since there are 10 departments, the number of senators is 30. The senators are elected for a period of 6 years and can be re elected with no term limits. The constitution stated that 1/3 of the senate must be replaced every 2 years. Article 96 deal with the requirements to be a senator.

Someone must be 30 years of age, never renounced to the Haitian nationality, not in prison while running for office, the person must reside in the department that is going to elect him for at least 4 consecutive years. There are other requirements that are not listed here in this paragraph. Articles 96 talks about the national assembly. The national assembly is simply the meeting of the two houses plus sometimes the invitation of the president, the government and the supreme court. The constitution clearly stated when parliament should meet in national assembly. Amending the constitution, the president oath of office, the prime minister declaring his or her program of government and many other situations require parliament to meet in national assembly.

Appointing and dismissing prime ministers

Appointing and dismissing prime ministers and other officials of the government have been a power granted to parliament by the constitution. The parliament has had the power to recall the president but for some reasons, the Haitian parliament has never recall a president in the history of the country. If parliament has done a such thing. I am not in knowledge of it. Article 129 gives parliament the power to recall the prime minister or any member of the government. Articles 185 and 186 clearly stated what should happen to the president, prime minister and the secretaries of state if they fail to do their job. Parliament has the power to removed them from office. The military government and the semi-presidential system set by the 1987 constitutions are two reasons why parliament has failed to recall a president from office.

The military government has created a cult of personality in the executive branch. Parliament has been intimidated by the presidency because the presidency usually gets the backing of the army. Even though president Jean Bertrand Aristide has put an end to the existence of the army, that cult of personality is still there. Another thing that will make it difficult for the parliament to remove the president from office is its popularity. In a semi-presidential system, the president is elected by the people. In Haitian political culture, the parliament cannot remove a popular president from office for wrong doing. If parliament attempts to do that and has some success, it can be a complicated situation between the state and the people of country.

The following prime ministers have been appointed by parliament and have been dismissed directly and indirectly by parliament. When I say indirectly, it means that pressure from parliament and the people of Haiti forces the prime ministers to resign. The names here may not be in order of date. I am just trying to show the instability in the system and how to fix it. Rene Garcia Preval has been prime minister of Haiti under the first JBA administration. He was easily appointed by parliament because of the popularity of the former priest. Unfortunately, President Aristide lasted less than a year in office because of the Coup D'Etat of September 30, 1991. The former prime minister went into exiled. While in exile, the president chose Robert Malval as prime minister. He was appointed by parliament and later on resign on his own because of political pressure from the people and the military government that existed at the time.

When Aristide returned to power in 1994 he had Smarck Michel and Claudette Werleigh for prime ministers. Smarck Michel was an industrialist and Claudette Weirleigh was a Diplomat of Career. Both were easily appointed prime ministers by parliament because of the popularity of Aristide. However, Aristide did not last long in office and the political pressure caused them to depart the government. Claudette Weirleigh was followed by Rosny Smarth in 1996 under the first Preval Administration. Rosny Smarth resigns the prime minister position in 1997 before the president was able to find someone to replace him. Rosny Smarth was followed by Jacques Eduard Alexis from 1999 to 2001. Jacques Eduard Alexis is a great intellectual with a lot of experience in the government. He only served two years in office.

During the second Preval presidency, Jacques Eduard Alexis became prime minister again and only served two years in office from 2006 to 2008. Political pressure from parliament and the people of Haiti over food prices among other things forced him to resign. Gerard Latortue Became prime minister during the second Coup D'Etat against President Jean Bertrand Aristide in 2004. He lasted about 2 years in office. He was a bureaucrat under the presidency of Leslie Francois Manigat in 1988. He was also a UN official. He organized the 2006 election that brought President Preval to his second presidency. Alexis resignation was followed by Michelle Duvivier Pierre Louis. She was the second woman to be prime minister of Haiti. She was Prime minister under Preval from 2008 to 2009. Before becoming prime minister, she was the director of an organization financed by US billionnaire George Soros. After Michelle Duvivier Pierre Louis, a series of prime ministers have followed that did not last long in office.

Organizing the senate and the Chamber of Deputies

Just like I said earlier, the Canadian Model where the member of the House of Commons are elected for five years and from different districts is a good example to follow. The larger a province or territory, the more people a province or territory has in Canada, the more are the senatorial districts and the districts for the house of common. We have to understand that Haiti is not Canada. We will have to alter things to fit our culture and society. For example, Haiti Has about 42 arrondissements, we will have one senator per arrondissement which will give the country 42 senators. Haiti has currently about 119 deputies representing different districts. All of them would be elected for five years in a direct election. The current configuration where the president of the chamber of deputies and the office of the prime minister are two separate positions is good and does not need any changes.

With the current political configuration, no prime minister last five years in office. It was either they resign on their own or parliament dismissed them. These people are good and qualified people that can help the country. With a shaky system, they cannot do much. As I am writing this book, some of these people are all over North America and Europe serving other governments or academic institutions. You might ask yourself why they do not stay in Haiti. My answer is that, the political environment does not give them the necessary conditions to stay and serve the country. People like Jacques Eduard Alexis is still in Haiti serving in the field of Education at Quisqueya University. There might be other former prime ministers still living in the country.

Former Prime minister and de facto president Marc L Bazin had a prime minister club that was consisted of former prime ministers of the country. They used to discuss the current situation in Haiti. No matter what someone thinks about Marc L Bazin, that was a good initiative. Bazin himself was the prime minister of Haiti from 1992 to 1993 after the coup d'etat that took Aristide out of the country. It was an initiative to encourage the former leaders to stay in the country. This is the way they do it in the Bahamas, Jamaica, Canada, Germany and many other countries with parliamentary government. If no party or coalition has that 2/3 majority the president would choose someone from the chamber of deputy and that person would become the prime minister of the country with the support of the chamber of deputy and the senate.

The government would be inside parliament not outside of it. The person chosen to be prime minister would choose his or her vice-prime minister. In case of death, resignation and other issues, the vice-prime minister would replace the prime minister without much controversy. The people would elect the parliament and the parliament would elect the president of the country from different candidates. The English Caribbean is a good example for us to follow. Canada, Germany, Italy, Trinidad and Tobago are good examples. We would create what I call a parliamentary government with Haitian characteristics.

2015 -2016 Parliamentary election

Parliamentary elections were held in Haiti on August 9, 2015, with a second round planned initially on October 25, 2015. Two-thirds of the Senate and all members of the Chamber of Deputies were up for election.

The second round of the parliamentary elections that has been suspended in 2015 took place in October 2016, along with the first round for a third of the Senate and the first round of the whole new presidential election.

According to international observers, early rounds of voting have experienced significant fraud, including people voting more than once due to failure of indelible ink, vote buying due to lack of secrecy, poor training of election workers, poor tracking of political parties, and other problems. This has resulted in the nullification of some results and scheduling of re-runs. The United States has withdrawn funding for the October 2016 round, though it financially supported previous rounds and observation by the Organization of American States.

The 99 members of the Chamber of Deputies are elected in single-member constituencies using the two-round system;. In March 2015 a new electoral decree stated that the new Chamber of Deputies will have 118 members, and the Senate will retain the 30 members.

On March 13, 2015, President Martelly issued a decree that split the Cerca La Source in two constituencies, and therefore increasing the number of deputies up to 119. One-third of the 30-member Senate is elected every two years, also using the two-round system. Like I said before, we need a parliamentary system of government such as the case in Italy where Senators and deputies are elected for five years in just one election with two rounds.

CHAPTER 10

THE EXECUTIVE AND THE MODELS OF GERMANY AND TRINIDAD AND TOBAGO

Germany and Trinidad and Tobago have what the political scientists called the parliamentary republic where the president is chosen by parliament. The government comes from the lower chamber. In Germany it is called the Bundestag and in Trinidad it is called the house of representative. Both mean the same thing. The prime minister is chosen among the members of the lower house. These two countries are great examples for us in Haiti. The bundestag of Germany was established by the basic law or the federal constitution of Germany in 1949 during the allied occupation after World War II. For the year 2021, it has 736 members that are elected every four years by the people of Germany.

Articles 134 to 172 deal with the executive branch. Here I am talking about the president and the prime minister. The constitution said that the president must be elected by the people and for the people. If there is a first election and there is no winner, a second election or a second round is held until someone has the majority vote to be the president of the country. The constitution mentions that the president is president for five years and he may not be re-elected after these five years. Some requirements to be president of Haiti include: be 35 years of age, have a piece of property in the country. The person has to be born in the Haiti and also have lived in the country for five consecutive years. The power of the president is listed clearly in the constitution.

Power to name the prime minister is one that presidents in Haiti exercise every now and then since prime minister come and go very quickly due to the weakness of the system. The prime minister is the head of the government. He must be chosen by the president of the country. He has the power to choose his ministers and the secretaries of state. Usually, he or she does that in concert with the president.

The presidency of Jean Bertrand Aristide

Since the writing of the 1987 constitution, these three presidents have made their impacts on the Haitian people more than any other presidents the country has had. Jean Bertrand Aristide was born in Port Salut, a city in the Sud department of Haiti. He grew up in Port Au Prince. He was educated at the College Notre Dame Du Cap which later on became Notre Dame University. In his academic career, Jean Bertrand Aristide has received his education in several countries such as: Israel, Greece, Dominican Republic, etc.

Just like many intellectuals of his time, Jean Bertrand Aristide was an anti-Duvalier. He was very famous for criticizing the government and also for his theology of liberation. After becoming a catholic priest, Jean Bertrand

Aristide started his politics in the ti legliz movements. The ti legliz or small church was his base for his campaign for a better Haiti for all. Aristide started preaching what Dr. Myles Munroe or Jesus Christ himself would call the gospel of the kingdom. That means God wants you to have food to eat, a good house to stay in, God wants you to have peace in your country, God wants you to be healthy and to enjoy a good economic system with the everlasting life.

For his first presidential campaign, Aristide joined with the FNCD or the Front National Pour le changement et la Democratie. I have mentioned that before in this book, FNCD was not a political party but a coalition that was trying to take power. Several political parties came together to create FNCD. FNCD leaders such as Victor Benoit, Evans Paul among others chose Aristide because of his popularity. Aristide won the election with more than 67% of the vote. That was for the first time in the nation's history a president has been elected by a such great majority. Unfortunately, the September 30, 1991 coup d'etat put an end to the joy and the celebration of the people. Raoul Cedras, Phillipe Biamby, Michel Francois and Emmanuel Constant were the leaders of that terrible Coup D'etat. I was in Port Au Prince at that time. It was a period of terror in the country.

Haiti was like a communist state that has rejected the existence of God. President Aristide returned to power in 1995 with the support of the Clinton Administration, the United Nations and other international institutions. He did not have much time to do much for the country. He organized the peaceful election that brought Preval to Power in 1995. The 2000 presidential election brought Jean Bertrand

Aristide back to power for a second term. Just like during his first term, president Aristide did not have the chance to finish his second term in office. An uprising in 2004 started by a former police chief named Guy Phillipe brought the presidency of Jean Bertrand Aristide to an end. He was force out of power to take refuge to Jamaica and later on in South Africa. On March 18, 2011, Jean Bertrand Aristide arrived in Port Au Prince from his exile in South Africa.

The presidency of Rene Garcia Preval

Rene Garcia Preval was born in Marmelade which is a commune or city in the Artibonite Department. He received his early education in Haiti and later on attended schools in Europe particularly Belgium and Italy. Preval father was an agronomist and work for president Paul Magloire. Preval followed in his father footstep and became an agronomist himself. After living in New York for about five years, Preval returned to Haiti and started working in several businesses. While in Haiti, his friendship with Aristide has given him the opportunity to become prime minister of the country. That opportunity to be prime minister has given him the opportunity to become president of the country during a period of ten years.

The executive branch fell under Preval who won the 1995 presidential election. He won more than 88% of the vote. Preval served a five year terms in office without interruption. Besides president Nissage Saget, Preval is the second president who has served a full term in office. Preval supported the philosophy of the Fanmi Lavalas party during his first term in office. He opposed the viewpoints of OPL in the Haitian parliament. Organisation du people en lutte or OPL is one of the main political party in the country. During the presidency of Preval major reforms have been made. Reforms in agriculture, schools and unemployment were visible to the people and that is why the people gave him a second term in office.

Rene Garcia Preval won the presidency for a second term in the 2006 presidential election. He broke with the Fanmi Lavalas party and started his LesPwa party or Hope. It was not easy for Preval to win the election although he was the most popular politician of the country at the time. He had some good success in his first term as president. He was able to use that effectively for the second term. Gerard Latortue, a former UN official was prime minister during that period. There were strategies to prove that Preval was not the winner of the election in 2006. The people of Haiti was not ready to accept a president that they did not vote for. They were ready to march and march and march until the CEP and the international community gave them what they want. That is exactly what happened. Rene Garcia Preval became president for a second term. Two years in the presidency of Preval, there was a food riot that he managed to survive. The people were marching for better conditions of living all over the country and Preval was not able to deliver what he promised the people.

Besides not being able to deliver, Preval has distance himself from Aristide. The people were not ready to forgive him for that. About two years after the food riot in the country, the most fatal earthquake in the country's history occurred. It was too much for president Preval to handle. People in Haiti and outside of Haiti criticized the president for his weak response to the earthquake. The arrival of the 2010-2011 election period has put an end to the presidency of Rene Garcia Preval. Under his leadership, the executive branch did not deliver much. In one occasion he was running the country without the most important power, that is the parliament. His distance from Aristide was his most severe critic from the people of Haiti.

The presidency of Michel Joseph Martelly

After the presidency of Rene Garcia Preval, the executive branch fell under the leadership of one of the most well-known and one of the most successful musician in the country, Joseph Michel Martelly. According to many, since the 1987 constitution has been put in effect, Michel Martelly was the third democratically elected president. Michel Martelly was born in a middle class family in Port Au Prince. The family was doing business in the oil industry with Shell. After high school, Martelly tried the military but did not stay for long. In 1984, he moved the United States and returned to Haiti one year later. That was when he started heavily in the Haitian music industry. Martelly's way of singing in plain creole has helped him in his celebrity status all over the country. During 1988 and onward, Martelly was the president of konpa mizik in Haiti.

In 1997, Martelly and Wyclef managed to work together and they have been successful in a music video. People who know the president before he was president reported that he has a lot of political views about what is going on in the country. They said that the only problem is that, his musical talents have prevented people to see how serious Martelly was about politics. In 1992 Martelly gave his participation by singing for free to protest the return of Aristide to power. In 2004, a good friend of Martelly became the prime minister and this time he returned to Haiti not to be part of the government under Gerard Latortue but to escape economic crisis in Miami on his properties.

Martelly who had a lot to say and to do about the politics of Haiti but never had a chance, participated in the 2010-2011 presidential election in the country. It was the perfect timing for the president since the most popular party in the country was not allowed to participate in the election. Here I am talking about Fanmi Lavas. Besides Fanmi Lavalas, the most popular politician in the early days of the race was not allowed to participate in the election. Basically the race was about Martelly and Mirlande Manigat. One problem with Mirlande Manigat is the fact that she has been in politics for years but was not as popular as she thought she was. Psychologically speaking, the ball was on Martelly side. As politicians in the United States like to say, Martelly has all the cards. Joseph Michel Martelly became president of Haiti in March 2011.

According to the people and according to what I saw, he is a very smart person and he has a strong will to advance the country. He managed to publish the 1987 amended constitution which requires that 30% of all government jobs go to women. He has terminated a few projects started by President Rene Garcia Preval. He went to the homes of all the former leaders of the country to create an atmosphere of Unity. These strategies have proven that if the political elite want to help, the country can go a long way. Some intellectuals criticized the president for publishing the amended constitution of 1987. If he did not publish it, he would have criticism. He published it, there are criticisms. I think the president has done the right thing by publishing the amended version of the constitution. Some parts of the amended constitution create more confusion.

Since we are in a constitutional period, I think we have to keep amending the constitution until it becomes a document that can serve efficiently the people of Haiti. It is better to try and fail than not to try at all. The president has tried and for the most part, he has failed. I personally give him credit for trying. That is what life and politics are all about.

As I have mentioned in several places in the previous chapters, the constitution of 1987 was a good thing. The only problem is that: we need to work on it to make it what it supposes to be to serve the people. The semi-presidential system it established is not going to remove the country from that economic and political predicament it is in. when it comes to the president, I am proposing to elect the president through a parliamentary vote such as the case in Trinidad and Tobago, Germany and Italy. The parliament would meet in a general meeting consisting of the two chambers. They would vote for the president in a two round election, if there is no winner in the first round. The current members of parliament should not be candidate in that election.

For the government, I have already mentioned that, it will come from the chamber of deputies. If there are for example 70 deputies, the government will be consisted of these 70 deputies or some of them as ministers and secretaries of state and other government officials. To be a member of the government, you have to be first a member of parliament. Close to us we have good example of this parliamentary system of government. The Bahamas, Jamaica, Dominica and Trinidad and Tobago are good examples to follow. The power of the chamber of deputy would be somewhat decrease and the power of the senate would be somewhat increase. The government would use a process that I call direct proportional representation. Here is what I mean, if a party such as Fanmi Lavalas has 40% of the chamber of deputy, it will have 40% of the government. If a party such as OPL has 30% of the chamber of deputy, it will have 30% of the government. If a party such as RDND has 20% of the chamber of deputy, it will have 20% of the government. It would be the same thing for the other parties present in parliament.

In this reform, the deputies would continue to be elected as usual and the sanator would be elected one per arrondissement. If we have 43 arrondissemts, we would have 43 senators. They would be directly elected by the people of the country such as the case in Italy. The traditional politics that have handicapped the country for decades because of a divided political system of government such as semi-presidential democracy or presidential democracy would be gone and be replaced by a parliamentary government with direct proportional representation.

The 2016 Presidential Election

Presidential elections were held in Haiti on 20 November 2016, after having been postponed several times. The elections were overseen by the Provisional Electoral Council (CEP), and were held using the two-round system, with a second round scheduled for January 29, 2017 if no candidate received an absolute majority of the votes in the first round (50% plus one vote). However, on November 27, 2017 election officials announced that, according to preliminary results, Jovenel Moïse had won the election in the first round with more than 50% of the vote. Voter turnout, in the election held 6 weeks after Hurricane Matthew hit Haiti, was reported to be 21%. Jovenel Moise won and assume office on February 7, 2017.

As a result of the massive protests after the 2015 election, the runoff originally scheduled to be held on December 27, 2015 was postponed several times, with the last one scheduled to be held in October 2016. However, the Conseil Electoral Provisoire (CEP) announced on April 5, 2016, that fresh elections would be held on October 9, with a possible runoff on January 8, 2017. The first round planned for October 9, was subsequently postponed due to the passage of Hurricane Matthew.

A total of 27 candidates ran for president, but only six actively campaigned and were seen as serious contenders: Edmonde Supplice Beauzile (Fusion Social Democrats), Jean-Henry Céant (Renme Ayiti, "Love Haiti"), Jude Célestin (LAPEH/Peace), Jean-Charles Moïse (Pitit Dessalines), Jovenel Moïse (Parti Haïtien Tèt Kale), and Maryse Narcisse (Fanmi Lavalas). Each of the six, except for Beauzile, "have had strong ties to one or more of the former elected presidents: Michel Martelly, René Préval and Jean-Bertrand Aristide."

CHAPTER 11

THE JUDICIARY AND THE CANADIAN JUSTICE SYSTEM MODEL

Canada is among the top ten countries with the best governments in the world. Its justice system which includes the court system, the police system and the prison system is well organized and decentralized. There are different types of court systems in Canada. The four main types are: the provincial court systems appointed by the provincial governments, the superior courts, the court of appeals and the supreme court of Canada appointed by the federal government. The court system is decentralized in Canada which creates a system of check and balance.

Article 173 to 184 deals with the Supreme Court or Cour de Cassation. The Supreme Court is one of the three main powers in the country. The constitution recognizes that and that is why the power of the judiciary is very important and cannot be overlook. Judges for the Supreme Court and Courts of appeal are appointed for 10 years and the judges of the courts of first instance and peace are appointed for 7 years. The constitution continues to say that the judges of the Supreme Court are appointed by the president from a list submitted by the senate and the judges of the courts of appeal, first instance and of peace are appointed from a list submitted by the departmental assemblies and the communal assemblies.

Addressing the justice system in Haiti is not an easy task to do because of the complexity of the problems of the country. In this chapter, I am giving the framework in which the system needs to operate. If you read this book carefully I talk more about the big picture than the details. That does not mean the details are not important. The details are as important as the big picture. I am just addressing what I have knowledge to address. A good justice system is good for the whole country. A good justice system creates the confidence of the people in the government. It also creates an atmosphere for economic and social development. In government, everything affects everything. That means if one institution is not working, it creates a weakness in the other institutions and makes them dysfunctional. This is what the justice system has done in the country.

We have to understand that our justice system is based on French and the American models. While I am not here criticizing these countries, we have to create a justice system based on Haitian characteristics. We can keep the main things based on the models of the French and the Americans but we have to reform the system to adapt to our political reality.

The Court system

Our justice system is based on the French model. I am not criticizing France here, but their model is very centralized and must be reformed. In Haiti, we can keep the basics of the French system but reform it according to our reality. In Haiti, the justice system is bankrupt for several reasons and in different aspects. For public opinion, judges, lawyers, government commissioners, etc. are corrupt. The reality is that we have corruption in every country in the world. The truth is to create a justice system that can fight corruption within itself. To create this system, decentralization is essential. The Haitian judicial system is divided into four levels: court of peace, court of first instance, court of appeal and court of cassation or CSPJ (Superior Council of the Judicial Power) According to the current format, the municipal government, the departmental government, the senate must submit their list of judges to the president for final choice. This system forces judges to make decisions in favor of one party or another or in favor of one president or another.

This system must be decentralized where the municipal government, the departmental government, the President of the Republic submit their list to the CSPJ for judicial investigation and the CSPJ to the Senate of the Republic for the final choice of judges. This is the case in the most democratic countries. For government commissioners, a percentage must be chosen by the national government and another percentage by the departmental governments for the better functioning of the state. Democratic processes such as elections have tested our justice system beyond belief. These first steps must be taken to at least alleviate the problem.

The Police System

There are two kind of police systems: centralized and decentralized. Centralized police is a police system with a lot of different units but one main director. The police system of France, Italy, Spain, Haiti, Russia, People's Republic of China, Chili, etc. are good examples. Decentralized police is a police system where each level of government has its own independent police force that work side by side. Instead of creating a lot of units under one main director, on many occasions, the government creates independent police forces based on the reality on the ground and based on the different levels of governments. The police systems of Canada, USA, United Kingdom, Japan, Germany are great examples of decentralized police systems. The United States and Canada have 10 to 15 different types of independent police systems. City police, sheriff police, state police or provincial police, federal police or investigative police, parliamentary police, Capitol police, Supreme court police, Presidential police, etc are well known in these two countries.

In Haiti, our police system must be done at four levels:

Municipal Police
Departmental police
National Police
Investigative Police or Judiciary Police

All we have to do is to reform the national police and transform it into these levels. For the **municipal or communal police**, we would have a post in each commune under the direction of the communal government. 50 to 60% of the national police force would go to the municipal police. Let's say there are 16,000 police officers in the National Police, of which 50 to 60% or 8,000 to 9,600 police officers would constitute the communal police services under the direction of the mayor and city council, something similar in Canada and the States -United. For the **departmental police**, we would have a post in each arrondissement under the direction of the departmental government. 20 to 25% of the national police force would go to the departmental police. Units such as circulation units, roads units, border units, etc can be part of the departmental police. Let us say that there are 16,000 police officers in the national police force, 15% or 1,900 to 2,400 police officers would constitute under the direction of the first delegate and the departmental assembly. For the **National Police**, we would have a post in each departmental capital. 30 to 40% of the national police force would remain in the national police with this new restructuring.

Let's say that there are 16,000 police officers in the national police force, of which 5, 000 to 7, 000 police officers would constitute the national police force under the direction of the Prime Minister and the Director of Police. Units such as: presidential units, legislative units, diplomatic units, border units, prison units, etc can still be part of the national police. **The Investigative Police** or DCPJ (Direction Centrale de la police Judiciaire) should be independent from the other police systems in order for the work to be done properly. It would supervise the works of the other police departments. It should have its own independent director under the leadership of the central government and the prime minister and the president of the country. 15% to 20% of the national police officers should go to the investigative police. Its primary role will be different types of investigations. Each level of police would have a specific level of responsibility. For examples, the municipal police will fight against gangs, kidnappings and other crimes, the departmental police will be the roads police. The national police will be the main police supporting the municipal and departmental police. It will also be the main police protecting the diplomats, the senators, deputies, judges, the prime minister of the country, the president of the country and other officials. Units that cannot be part of the municipal and departmental police will be in the national police. Units such as: prison police, border police, diplomatic police, coast guard police, etc will be in the national police. These numbers here are not exact. It is just to give you an idea on how we can decentralize our police system.

The Prison System

You must understand that in any organized country, the prison system is key to the proper functioning of government or state. It seems that Haitian politicians have lost the responsibility of forming prisons for the country's public safety. There are a lot of criticisms about the prison system in Haiti. One of the criticisms of the Haitian prison is overcrowding where the accused and the convicted are in the same cell. According to research and a report by RNDDH (National Human Rights Defense Network), Haiti has more prisoners than it has jails or prisons. More than 70% of prisoners do not have the chance to appear before a judge on their case. Many prisoners die of malnutrition and lack of health. Like The State, the Justice system and the Police, the first thing to do and to simplify the problem, is to decentralize the prisons in Haiti into two levels: **Departmental prisons** under the control of the departmental government for inmates serving 2 years or less and **National prisons** under national government for inmates serving 3 years or more. For example, we would have a prison in each arrondissement for departmental prisons and a prison in each department for the national prisons. Prisons for women, military, young people, etc. would be of this model. This prison model is a success in Canada and the USA in a structural way.

The Judiciary and Ertha Pascal Trouillot

According to the 1987 constitution, if the president is unable to fulfill his or her duties while in office, the president of the Supreme Court will have to take power and lead the country. The judges or the justices of the supreme court enjoy that type of power. That is why it is important for the justices of the country to be qualified and be ready to be president in case something unexpected happens to the president. The amended version of the 1987 constitution has managed to change that. Based on the new system, if the president is unable to fulfill his or her duty while in office, the prime minister has to replace the president for the remaining time of the presidency. The question is what if, there is no prime minister at the moment. What if the prime minister is recalled by parliament and before choosing a new prime minister, the president died. I believe it was a good thing to try to amend the constitution but we have a long way to go. That is why I believe firmly unless we cross that constitutional period, nothing significant will happen in Haiti.

Ertha Pascal Trouillot was born in 1943 in Petionville, Port au Prince, Haiti. She grew up with 9 siblings in the Port Au Prince area. Ertha was a teenager when Francois Duvalier took power. When Francois Duvalier opened the Francois Duvalier high school in Petion Ville, it was a great opportunity for her because she had met the requirements to attend the school. In that public school, she met, her future husband Ernst Trouillot. At first Ertha wanted to go to medical school but her boyfriend of the time, Ernst Trouillot suggested Law. She did not fight over the issue and listen to her boyfriend at the time. Ertha Pascal Trouillot studied law at the school of Law of Gonaives in Artibonite, Haiti. She has had a successful career in the Haitian justice system before becoming the Supreme Court judge.

In 1988, she was the first woman to be elected to the Supreme Court. She lost her husband during that period but she did not let that put her moral down. She was a strong voice for the voiceless women of her time. She raised her daughter to the best of her ability. According to many, she was pure in a corrupt system. That was a very difficult thing to do in a country basically run by military governments for more than 150 years. She had all kind of political connections with the highest political leaders of the country at that time.

The government of president Prosper Avril was ousted by a coup d'etat in 1990, general Herard Abraham took over the presidency for three days and later on handed power to Ertha Pascal Trouillot in 1990. The first female president had the big duty of organizing democratic elections all over the country. She managed to organize the first democratic election in Haiti. Aristide won the presidency by more than 67% of votes. Ertha has proven the power of the judicial branch to give justice to whom justice is due.

Before Ertha, no one was able to organize a such peaceful and democratic election. The great thing about it, is that, the forces of the international community were not that strong in Haiti. If the International community was in Haiti, most of the credit of the election would go to them. While I am very respectful for the works of the International community, Ertha and the CEP in 1990 have proven that if given a good chance, Haiti can organize itself and women have more to deliver to the country than men think.

The Judiciary and Emile Jonassaint

Emile Jonassaint was a judge in the Haitian justice system. He was born in Port De Paix, lived most of his life in Port au Prince, attended school there and also died in that city. After the September 30, 1991 Coup D'Etat, the military offered the job of being president to Emile Jonassaint who did not say no to a lifetime opportunity for many Haitian politicians. As far as the Clinton Administration was concerned, JBA was the president of the country. The United States, the UN and other institutions were putting enough pressure to the Jonaissaint government to resign so Jean Bertrand Aristide can come back to power. The government was in power for about five months before surrender to the pressure of the international community. It was not an easy job for the Clinton Administration to do. Just before the surrender, president Clinton sent the former president of the United States, Jimmy Carter to negociate Aristide return with President Emile Jonaissaint and the military regime led by general Raoul Cedras. After President Jimmy Carter, the Clinton Administration sent General Collin Powell and senator Sam Nunn to negociate the Return of Aristide.

The military regime along with President Emile Jonassaint had realized they did not have any option but to give up power. A lot of people have criticize Emile Jonassaint for taking power during that time. We have to understand that he found himself in a difficult situation. According to the 1987 constitution, he was next in line for power since he was from the supreme court. According to many observers, Emile Jonassaint was very cooperative in transferring power to the elected leader of the country Jean Bertrand Aristide.

The Judiciary and Alexandre Boniface

Alexandre Boniface was born in 1936. He was raised in Port Au Prince. He attended law school and worked in the Haitian justice system for about 25 years. He was appointed to the supreme court of the country by president Aristide in 1990. Most people reported that he was known for fairness in a corrupt justice system. The uprising that would lead to the coup d'etat of October 2004 made it difficult for Aristide to remain in power. After Jean Bertrand Aristide has left the country for Jamaica in 2004, Boniface Alexandre became president of Haiti. Boniface Alexandre worked with the international community to maintain peace in the country after the departure of Aristide. It was not an easy thing to do because of the supporters of Aristide. The presidency of Boniface Alexandre was more ceremonial than active. Most of the power of the country was in the hand of prime minister Gerard Latortue. Boniface Alexandre along with prime minister Gerard Latortue organized the election that would lead president preval to his second presidency.

CHAPTER 12

THE MUNICIPAL, DEPARTMENTAL GOVERNMENTS AND THE FRENCH / SOUTH AFRICA MODELS

The decentralization process

Decentralization is key for political development, public security and economic development for any country and Haiti is no exception. When talking about decentralization, there are three main aspects that we have to focus on: Institutionalized Decentralizaion, which is the process of transferring power to newly created institutions and is different from the act of deconcentration of power, which is the transfer of power within the same institution. This decentralisation is general in nature and affects all policies or powers related to the territory or targeted to specific areas of public policy and government.

Territorial Decentralization, this aspect of decentralisation is geared to giving the territorial collectivities in Haiti separate defined responsibilities and resources and to provide for the election of representatives by the inhabitants of those territories. Again this is different from deconcentration, which is when the central government aims to improve efficiency by delegating certain policy and powers to a centrally nominated representative or a departmental delegate. Functional Decentralization, this aspect of decentralisation takes place when central or local government decides not to directly carry out one of its powers but to transfer the power to a public body such as a departmental council or a Mairie.

France and South Africa have one of the best decentralized government in the world. It is true that France is not as decentralized as the USA, Canada or Germany but they have done a great job in at least decentralize the government or the state. France still has the prefect system which is a system where the central or national government appoints commissioners at the departmental and regional levels. This prefect system will not work in Haiti and will contribute to centralization and the dysfunction of the country. For example, each department in France is divided into districts that vote for people in the departmental assembly for six years. These departmental politicians vote for a president for 6 years. The president chooses his cabinet from among the members of the departmental assembly to form his government. Just like in France, South Africa has done a great job in decentralizing the country at least politically. At the municipal level, the people vote for the municipal council and the municipal council chooses the mayor among its members.

At the provincial level, the people of the province vote for the provincial assembly and the provincial assembly chooses the prime minister of that province among its members.

These two countries do not leave any room for populists to come and run the country with no vision and no plan. Just like in South Africa, in Haiti, we do not have to directly vote for the mayor or the delegate or the president. We can indirectly vote for these positions to avoid comedians and populist politicians with no plan from running the country.

Articles 76 - 84 deal with the organization of the departmental government. Besides the country, the department is the largest territorial division in the country. Some departments in Haiti have more people than some countries in the Caribbean. Let's take for example the Bahamas. Le Nord or the North has more people than the Bahamas. The constitution said that, each department must be governed by a departmental council made up of 3 people elected by the municipal council for a period of five years. These people running the department should not necessarily be member of the departmental assembly according to the constitution.

The constitution continues to give the requirements for someone to be a member of the departmental council. You have to be at least 25 years of age, live in the department for 3 years and that person has never been in jailed or sentenced for crimes and other related activities. Government officials have the power to attend the meeting of the departmental council. People such as senators and deputies of the departments, people of the civil society and people that are working on behalf of the department but are not directly part of the government. According to the constitution, when it comes to the plan of the department, that must be done in cooperation with the central or national government. The department cannot set up its own program.

Without the central government support, the departmental program cannot succeed. In case the departmental council or the departmental assembly is not working efficiently, the central government can intervene to support the departmental government in whatever way possible. Based on the constitution, if the departmental government is dissolved, the central government has the power to appoint a commission until election is organized by the permanent electoral council.

The delegate

According to article 185, the delegates and vice delegates are appointed by the central government to ensure everything is running smoothly in the department. That system must be changed. the delegate and the vice delegate should be chosen from among the members of the departmental assembly. Let's say the departmental assembly has 30 members from 30 voting districts in the department, the president would choose someone from the 30 people in the departmental assembly in case the members are unable to choose their leader. That person would give his or her governmental plan for the department to the departmental assembly. If the departmental assembly support the plan and it does not interfere with the central government program in a bad way, it should take effect.

Just like the governors in the United States, departmental presidents in France and the prime ministers of the provincial governments in Canada, that delegate would have strong power to appoint his or her departmental secretaries from the members of the departmental assembly. He would have the power to hire and fire them. Firing them does not mean that they are no longer member of the departmental assembly. In the provincial government of Quebec, someone can be a member of the provincial legislature and not being part of the government. Since I call for proportional representation where all the parties that are present in the departmental assembly must be part of the government, there will not be room for traditional partisan politics. The spirit might still be there but it will be very small since all the parties or coalitions are part of the government. Think for a moment of the power that the constitution gives a prime minister.

The same power should be given to the delegate at the departmental level. The only difference is, he or she would not be allowed to sign international treaty or traveling to meet foreigners in the name of the national government because he or she does not represent the national government.

Organizing the departmental government is very central and important. Until we organize the departmental government, the process calls decentralisation is not going to work. President Martelly was very interested in decentralizing the departmental governments. The presidents before him were very much interested in the development of the departments. What you and I have to remember is: we are in a constitutional period in our history. Unless the necessary changes are made in the constitution, we will never get where we want to be as a country. Some politicians just think that, they can just bypass the constitutional reforms that are needed to develop the department and have success. They are wrong.

The problems in the constitution have to be addressed first. In this book, I call for a parliamentary system of government to take Haiti out of this problem or this predicament. We have a lot of examples of parliamentary governments that are functioning in the Caribbean and around the world. One of my best example for Haiti is France at the municipal, departmental and regional level. There is also the example of Canada. In Canada, there is the central or federal government and the provincial governments. In Canada, there are about 5 main political parties. When it comes to the provincial government, here is how it is organized: Let's take for example Quebec.

Quebec is the largest province in Canada and its capital city is Quebec City and its largest city is Montreal. The national assembly of Quebec has about 125 members elected by the people of Quebec from 125 voting districts or what they call in the English system riding. The 125 voting districts vote 125 representants in the national assembly. The party or coalition with the most vote form the government. That party chooses the premier or prime minister of quebec from the member of the national assembly not from the outside. As I am writing this book, the current prime minister of quebec or premier of Quebec is Pauline Marois who just replaced Jean Charest in the recent election. Let's say for example, le Departement de L'Ouest has 105 communal sections in its 20 communes or cities. The government can regroup these 105 communal sections into for example 50 voting districts.

During the election period, the people would go to vote

for the departmental assembly. The people would elect 50 members of the departmental assembly. The party or coalition with the 2/3 majority in the departmental assembly would be required to form the government with proportional representation which means that all the party present in the departmental assembly must be part of the government. In case there is no party with the 2/3 majority, the president of the country would select a member from the departmental assemblies with the support of the departmental assembly, that person would become the delegate of the department and that delegate would choose his or her vice delegate for a period of five years since the departmental assembly just like the parliament would be elected for a period of five years. That system of electing members of the departmental assembly from the municipal assembly is not working and will never work.

The system of the president choosing a delegate outside of the departmental assembly will never work. The constitution talks about the interdepartmental council in articles 87. That interdepartmental council is made up of 10 members representing the 10 departments of the country. Once the constitution is amended, there will not be any need for the interdepartmental council. The senate would have to supervise the work of the departmental government or assembly and report to the president of the country. Let's take for example education, the senate education committee would supervise the work of the education committee in the departmental assembly and report to the senate and the senate report to the president. The education committee in the departmental assembly would report to the education committee in the chamber of deputy.

The best way to understand what I am trying to say her is to understand the French model and the Canadian model. If you go make some research on Canada or France, you will have a better understanding of what I am trying to say here. Setting up a departmental tax and a national tax would help greatly in the development of the department. The departmental tax would stay in the department for economic and social development while the national tax would go to the central government for the programs of the national government. Let's take for example education. The departmental government and the national government can have an agreement where the primary schools and the secondary schools are built by the departmental governments while the technical schools and the universities are built by the national government.

Departmental institutions such as the prison system, the police system, public education, etc are key in the autonomy of the departments. We have to change the system. The officials of the departmental governments will have a budget for five years in the department and said to the central government, here is what we have and here is what we need. The good thing about this new system is that: the departmental government can set up a fund where people from that particular department can send money. For example, people from the Artibonite department living in Canada can send money for development in Artibonite. The process would be the same for the remaining departments of the country.

The French model of municipal government works just

like the departmental government. The different district of the commune vote for the communal assembly and the assembly choose a president for six years that becomes the mayor. All countries have local governments. In the Caribbean, every single country has local governments. Small Caribbean country such as Puerto Rico and Dominica have local government. Big Caribbean countries such as Cuba and Dominican Republic have local government. What about our friends in the North: the United States and Canada? They both have local governments. In Haiti the word local government does not use but the word Mairie or Meri or La commune or the city.

In the United States, the history of communal governments or county governments started in the 17th century. The companies that were responsible to bring the wealth of the New world to Europe would settled in a place and gives it a name. whatever the name was, that was the name of the city. Just like in Biblical times, if for example the Dessalines is settled in a place, they will call that place Dessalines. Here I am just giving you an example. In Virginia, a group of businessmen from Europe settled in a place and called that plane Jamestown in the name of King James of England and call the State Virginia in the name of the virgin queen of England called Marie. After the American Revolution, the federal government worked with the state governments and the state governments started issuing charters to the county governments and make them more organizational.

During the 19th century, most municipalities in the United States were considered as corporations. Just like in the early days of the republic. One of the reason for that is that, companies were sent to develop cities. These companies were known as developers. Even today, a lot of companies specialize themselves in developing cities. I used to go to college in Virginia. I used to ride the Greyhound bus back and forth. One thing I have realized is that, the country called the United States is empty. People who live in the city do not realize that the country is empty. People living in Miami, New York, Los Angeles, Dallas and other big cities in the nation who have never drive, from one state to the next or from one city to the next, think the country is overcrowded. That is not the case at all.

Today, four main type of government exist in the United States: Town, City or county government, state and federal or national. Everything starts with a developer or a corporation. In the United States constitution, the tenth amendment makes the organization of local government the responsibility of the state government. The organization of city government in the Canada, follow the same path as the United States. As a matter of fact, the people call Canadians where Americans who moved to the North in their refusal of fighting against the British empire before the war of Independence of the United States. During the middle of the 19th century, laws were passed by the legislature of different provinces to organize the city governments with more efficiency such as boundaries, taxes and the type of institutions that should exist in a city to make it operational.

Before the 19th century, everything started with corporations searching for wealth in the names of the kingdoms of Europe such as France and England. During the 20th century, a lot of municipal reforms were made in

Canada to make city government better and more efficient. Just like in the United States, today the 4 main types of governments that exist in Canada are: town, city, provincial and national or federal.

The constitution and communal governments

Articles 66 to 74 deal with the communal governments. According to the constitution, each municipality is administered by a council of three members elected by the people of that municipality in a general election. The council is assisted in its work by a communal assembly or municipal assembly made up, of 1 person per communal section. The communal government is set for 4 years. Just like in the other branches of the government, the requirements are: be Haitian, the person must be 25 years of age, enjoy civil and political rights and never has been sentenced for serious crimes in the country. Based on the constitution, the communal government can be dissolved.

In that case, the departmental government or the national government must call the Permanent Electoral council to organize elections as soon as possible. Here I am not going to be too critical of the communal government even though they are not what they supposed to be. I sincerely believe that, if we can fix the government at the national level where we have a parliamentary government. That means the people elect the parliament and the parliament elect the president and the prime minister. If we fix the departmental government where the chief delegate or departmental prime minister is chosen from among the members of the departmental assembly and that departmental assembly must be elected by the people and not from the communal assembly. The rest of the problem would not be too significant after these changes. Communal institutions such as the fire department, the municipal police, etc are key in the autonomy of the communes.

I sincerely believe that the French model where the people of the commune vote for the communal assembly and the communal assembly chooses the mayors, vice mayors, etc among its members is the best form of city government. This model would be a great success if applied in Haiti. The city of Paris and the city of Pretoria in South Africa are great examples of this model of city government.

CHAPTER 13

ECONOMIC DEVELOPMENT IN HAITI AND THE AMERICAN INDUSTRIAL MODEL

The American industrial model follows a very simple pattern and very effective: American businesses, foreign businesses, New Entrepreneurs and decentralization. Decentralization simply means having a business in many places at once. For example, Amazon exists in many states and cities of the United States of America and countries at the same time. Delimart, Royal Oasis and large Haitian companies and foreign companies such as Best Western Hotel and Mariott Hotel can exist in all the ten departments and major cities of Haiti at the same time. This creates more job opportunities develop the economy and the country faster. 70 to 80% of jobs in America are created by small and big businesses of the country. 20 to 30 % of jobs in America are created by foreign businesses directly or indirectly. 5 to 10 % of jobs are created by new entrepreneurs. This book is more concentrate on the Political aspect of the Haitian crisis than the economic side of it. Both sides are important. One affects the other. I am more concerned about the political side because I am more knowledgeable in it. My passion to address the political side is more. It is just like wet and water. You cannot have one without the other.

I recently wrote an article in the Haitian Newspaper, Le National titled: Political decentralization and economic development in Haiti. More than 4 thousand people have read this article about the crisis. Most of the readers are in Haiti. This is to prove that a lot of people are still interested in seeing changes in the country in spite of this difficult moment. After stabilizing the country politically, at least three things must be done to bring economic changes in the country:

Protecting and promoting the Existing businesses that are present in the country

In this chapter, I am talking about all kind of businesses: Government, local Haitians, Diaspora and the international community. We cannot develop Haiti economically without this first step. The government of the country has to find a way to prevent people from burning and destroying businesses during strikes and marches in the country. A lot of jobs are being destroyed everyday by the insecurity situation in Haiti. Companies are shutting down their doors every day and live Haiti to go somewhere else. This must be stopped. We cannot speak about new investment in a country that cannot create the peaceful condition for the existing businesses to exist in the country.

Dimitri Vorbe recently declared that it is easier to do businesses anywhere in the Caribbean than in Haiti. This man is Haitian and wants to help his country by creating employment opportunities. In Haiti being rich means a negative thing. That must be stopped. Rich people bring inspiration for others. Let's think about the billionaires in America, they give away a lot of money and create a lot of opportunities. The richer the economic elite is in Haiti, the better it is for the economy. For the year 2017 – 2018, the famous Haitian newspaper Le Nouvelliste published a list of 200 companies in Haiti that pay taxes. Let's say that each company has 500 employees. That's a total of 100 thousand jobs.

You might say, that is not a lot but it is a lot for the people who provide for their families through these companies. Businessman Reginald Boulos told Valery Numa from Radio Vision 2000, he created jobs for 5 thousand people in the country. If 200 businessmen do the same thing, that is a million people, a million Haitians in the work force. I think that is a good analysis.

Existing businesses that are present outside of the country

Recently I was on the website of Fortune Global 2000. This is the list of the 2000 most powerful companies or corporations in the world. These companies are ready to do businesses in Haiti. I cannot say all of them are ready but some of them are ready. As a matter of fact, a lot of them are already in the country. Here I am more concerned about the ones that are not yet present in the country. President Martelly managed to open Marriott and Best western in the country.

That was a great business opportunity for the country. If the security situation was not deteriorating, these two companies could have brought many more in the country. If we manage to bring 500 of the 2000 global corporations in Haiti to invest that would be a big international success.

If the political leadership knows what it is doing in Haiti, 3 out of every 10 jobs could be related by foreign investment or outside investment. A lot of businesses of the Diaspora are ready to go and invest money, creating employment opportunities for the country. More than $ 2 billion dollars is sent annually to Haiti by the Diaspora. A lot of this money is sent by Haitians who own businesses all over North America and Europe. These people could have easily help creating jobs if public security was not a luxury in the country.

New entrepreneurs

In the United States, at least 2 million people create their own job every year. Let's say that the 2 million people have at least 5 employees to assist them, that is 7 million people in the labor market or the work force. If in Haiti, we have 10 thousand Haitians creating their own jobs every year and have 5 employees, it is 60 thousand people in the work force. New entrepreneurship is a great strategy for the government to make economic ideas become reality. The Haitian people are talented people. For the last 30 years, the country has known only broken governments with no real solution for the economic situation of the country. The people in Haiti find ways to survive in spite of that. Think for a moment if there is political stability in the country and the government is encouraging new entrepreneurship. That can revolutionize the country in a very good way. The better the existing businesses are doing, the more attractive it will be for the businesses that exist outside of the country to come in. The more they come in, the more the spirit of new entrepreneur will be in the country.

This is the domino effect. This affects the other. I have said it before and I will say it again, with public insecurity and broken governments, economic development in Haiti will not work. They are all related and connected together. We can take any industrial country, they all have political stability and a great economic environment for new ideas to emerge.

With Government reforms, Capitalism, socialism and Privatization will all work in Haiti

Economic ideologies have ruled the world since the beginning of time. Political ideologies and economic ideologies are husband and wife. They need each other. One cannot exist without the other. Show me a country with economic power, I will show you the same country with political stability. Show me a country with political stability and I will show you the same country with economic power. Even though political stability comes before economic possibilities, that does not mean one is more important than the other. If a country is stable politically and there is not economic development, that political stability will be transformed into political instability. If a country has good economic standing and there is no political stability, that economy will soon vanish.

Capitalism, socialism and privatization are some of the

most common terminologies used in talking about the economic system of any country today. Here, I am just trying to keep things simple. To me, a great teacher or a great professor is someone who keeps things as simple as possible. Economic ideologies go beyond the three mentioned here. Mercantilism, communism, market economy, mixed economy, agrarian economy, gift economy, etc. are all part of the package.

Capitalism

Once we see capitalism, we see capital or money. In America, there is a saying that stated: Time is money". That means nobody has time to waste. You have to be busy doing something that will bring you some money with your time. We can say time is capital or time is capitalism. Capitalism is not a collective ideology. It is a personal ideology or a private ideology. That is why greed is a very common word and a very accepted word in capitalistic society such as the United States. It is me, myself and I. Personal profit is the ultimate driving force behind this economic system. Competition in capitalism only benefits one person or a few people not the whole country. That is why a rich country such as the United States have so many poor people and homeless people living in it. In capitalistic societies, wealth and profits are way more important than the employees who produce them. In a capitalistic society, whoever can sell something for less money, will have more customers.

Walmart Corporation has more customer than Publix Corporation because Walmart finds a way to sell its products at a lesser price than Publix. In a capitalist society, if the government is not well organized and strong, the economic system will take over the political system. We see that clearly with the election of president Donald J Trump. A billionaire becomes the president of the United States. President Trump is not the only one. Most of the United States senators, governors, mayors, Congressmen and Congresswomen are millionaires. The well- known American Public speaker known under the name of Chris Hedges, call it: A coup d' etat in slow motion. This is where corporate America takes over the government of the country.

This is the result of uncontrolled capitalism. When the economic sector indirectly takes over the government, there is no government to defend the poor or the less fortunate. This is called economic exploitation. Capitalism does not like regulation. That is why the rich love to indirectly take over the government so there will be no regulation. Another word for NO REGULATION is Laissez Faire. This is where the government let the corporations do whatever they want. They exploit as many people as they want with no consequences. As long as they are paying some taxes to the government, everything is fine. If the government can control capitalism such as the case in Germany, Canada and the Scandinavian countries, this ideology can do a lot of goods. What you and I have to realized is that: the word in itself is not bad. It is not bad on a personal level to love capitalism. It becomes bad, when we do not see the whole country.

This is where capitalism if not controlled cannot help in the situation in Haiti. That is why I am proposing political reforms first then economic reforms. With good political reforms, Capitalism will work just fine in Haiti. For the last 30 years, the United States has not made any major political reforms. They have renovated buildings and build expressways but they have not made any major political reforms. That is why capitalism in the US is such a bad word. It means: Exploitation, corruption and Greed. France has been the leading country in political reforms for the last 30 years according to my research. In France, Capitalism works better than in the United States not because it is a different system over there but because of political reforms by the government.

Socialism

In socialism, we see society, in society we see community, we see people, we see the Masses, etc. It is an economic ideology where the people of the community or the people of the country own the economy. Some people love to say that socialism is a political ideology, it is not. Political ideology is different from economic ideology. Democracy is a political ideology not an economic ideology. Mixing things, will bring confusion. I am trying to avoid that in this book and in this chapter. In China, it is: People's Republic of China, People's Bank, People's Daily News, etc. Everything is done or everything is organized in the name of the People. I love that. With socialism, China and India have taken more people out of poverty in the last 30 years than the population of the United States, Mexico and Canada combined.

This is how powerful this economic ideology is. Americans Politicians and CEOs have done all they can to make socialism a bad word in the last 50 years, they have all failed. Senator Bernie Sanders, one of the smartest politician in America in the last 30 years run his campaign on a socialist ideology. It is an ideology where the people the United States come first. To me, it is a good ideology. In socialist countries such as People's Republic of China, Vietnam and Cuba, the government owns some of the means of production. Some of the big companies are owned by the government. This is called Dirigisme or State capitalism. Basically, the state or the government decides on some issues related to the economy. In socialist countries such as: Canada, Germany and Japan, private entities run the economy with strong government supervision.

Just like Capitalism will never work in countries with broken government or political instability, socialism will never work in countries with broken government and political instability. Politicians love to put their people or their friends or their family members in some key positions in the economy when they are in power. If they are in power for 2 years, they will try to put people in some key positions for that period of time. When they are kicked out of power, their people also are kicked out of their key positions. In a socialist economy where the leadership is changing constantly is not good for the economy. That is what has happened in Haiti for the last 30 plus years. That is why the government is unable to offer the basic services to the people of the country.

Privatization

When people hear the word privatization, it means a lot to them. In countries with socialist economies, the government owns a lot of the means of production. With political instability, the government is unable to deliver the services that the people deserve. Instead of the government running an electricity company for example, it let the private sector runs it for better management and for better services. Sometimes, people from the public sector or people from the government are unable to deliver the quality services that the private sector is able to deliver. That is just a fact. Some countries do not have political instability but let the private sector runs part of their economy for better result. Some people call privatization deregulation or public private partnership.

Whatever the name, it still means the transfer of an enterprise from the government to the private sector. Teleco in Haiti was founded in 1927 under the presidency of Louis Borno as a telegraph company. From 1927 to 2007, this is 80 years of service. During that 80 years, Teleco has not delivered much to the people in Haiti in term of telecommunication services. During the second presidency of Mr. Rene Preval from 2006 to 2011, Teleco was privatized with a Vietnamese based company known as Natcom. In less than 10 years, Natcom has delivered more services to the people of Haiti than Teleco in 80 years. I cannot forget Digicel who has entered the Market and has changed the game. That simply means privatization works. There is a good way to do it and there is a bad way to do it. President Preval has chosen the good way.

The president has chosen a rich foreign company instead of a poor local one. The bad way to do it, is: Letting a local company with no financial backbone taking over a government agency. When a private enterprise takes over a public enterprise, it has to have financial strength sometimes to invest in that government agency for better results in production. A government cannot afford to privatize a public company to a poor private company. That does not work. Government officials such as Yves Bastien, Charles Castel among others have done a great job in helping the government in that process. Haiti still have some major problems with the electric utility company called ED'H. we can still follow the example of Teleco. The country just need some good leadership to proceed. I am here saying: with good political reforms, capitalism, socialism and privatization can work in Haiti. No country is completely capitalistic or socialistic or privatized. It is a mixture of all of them sometimes. You just need good government and political stability for the economy to benefit everyone.

The Scandinavian countries are great successes and inspirations for the developing countries around the world. Their secret is good government reforms, small population and adaptation. Their unicameral parliament systems will not work in Haiti. Two chambers parliament or bicameral parliament is the best model for Haiti. The Scandinavian socialist economic programs will work very well in Haiti. Sweden, Denmark and Norway have a mixture of capitalism, socialism and privatization and everything seems to work very well. Their secret is good governments and good political systems that fit their cultures.

Five year plans for Haiti

The five year plans are a series of economic planning developed first in the former Soviet Union to boost industrial production of that former country to make it ready before the second World War. In the former Soviet Union there were about 13 different plans. Each plan addresses specific goals to be accomplished in a period of five years or before that. This is a very simple process but it was very effective. Through the five year plans, Joseph Stalin and the leadership of the former Soviet Union did manage to turn the Soviet Union which was an agrarian society to an industrialized country. The USSR was second industrial power after the United States. If the country did not collapse in 1991, it would have replaced the USA as the number one economic power in the world. To use the five year plans in Haiti, it will be very simple.

Remember in chapters: 3, 4 and 5, we talk about the different political regimes that exist in a democracy and I propose, the parliamentary system of government. I also mention that the presidential system of government and the current semi presidential system of government that is in the country will never work. This means, you cannot apply a five year plans in a presidential system of government or a semi presidential system of government. There will not be any continuity after the president live office. There are too much political confusions and political instability in these two system for the five year plans to develop. In this system, the parliamentary system, the parliament would be set for five years. The government would come from the members of parliament just like in Canada.

Once the prime minister gives his or her speech of his government program to parliament and it is approved, it will be for five years, regardless if the prime minister himself is dismissed after for example 2 years. There will be a first five year plan, a second five year plan, a third five year plan, etc. You have to realize if every prime minister appointed is coming with a new program of government, the country will never be developed. The reason I am saying that, is because in a lot of situations, the prime minister does not last 1 year or 3 years.

Five year plans in People's Republic of China, India and Vietnam

In spite of all the criticism of the five year plans, this is the greatest economic plan of all time. It has achieved more than the US New Deal and the Marshall plan in term of economic prosperity and opportunity. The United States and some other western countries did criticize the plan but were unable to stop its spread. People's Republic of China and Vietnam are still using the five year plans today after learning it from the former USSR. People's Republic of China is currently in its 13th plan from 2016 to 2020. Each plan addresses a specific part of the economy that is achievable in five year or less. Because of the five year plans, China is about to replace the USA as the number one economic power in the next 10 years according to some studies. China has lift more than 600 million people out of poverty in the last 30 years with the help of the five year plans. This is more than the population of the United States, Canada and Mexico combined.

India has known 12 plans all together. They discontinue the five year plans in 2017. According to many economists and political analysts, this is a big mistake. Why discontinue something that is working and working pretty well. It does not make any sense. Internal political division in the Indian Parliament is a big reason for that. Even though India is a stable democracy, internal politics is very strong in that country. Before discontinuing the five year plans, India has made significant progress. More than 200 million people were lift out of poverty with the help of the five year plans in India. This is more than half of the population of the United States. Vietnam has made significant progress with the five year plans. Together there has been 10 five year plans in Vietnam and the last one is 2016 to 2020. The livelihood of the Vietnamese people has greatly impacted in a positive way by the plans.

Vietnam has lift at least 40 million people out of poverty in the last 30 years with the five year plans. It looks like China and Vietnam will keep the plans for sometimes to come. According to United Nations statistical papers, more than 70% of the people that were lifted out of poverty in the last 30 years come from China, India and Vietnam. What is their secret? The five year plans and parliamentarism. In the People's Congress in China, in the National Assembly of Vietnam and in the parliament of India, that is where the major political and economic decisions are made. These countries do not believe in one man show government such as the case in the United States, Brazil, Mexico and our country Haiti. They believe in strong institutions instead of fake politicians with sweet lips.

Once political reforms are made in Haiti, the five year plans will be a great help. We need this plans. All poor countries need this plans. Africa needs this plans. In Haiti, we have to resist the critics, make the political reforms and apply this beautiful plans for a better Haiti for all.

CHAPTER 14

THE HAITIAN DIASPORA

The Haitian diaspora is one of the main forces of the country. It is a force that is not present in the country but it is there. People who visit Haiti who are not Haitians may think that it is not there but it is there. It is an invisible force that is impacting Haitians every day in the nation. The Haitian diaspora is the sustaining economic force of the nation. If the diaspora was not there, things would be more difficult in the country. When the international community gives money to Haiti, that money does not go directly in the hands of the people. Most of that money goes to the NGOs and government institutions. When the people outside of the country send money, that money goes directly to the people and therefore, they are able to start a small business, sending their children to school and helping their neighbors.

It is estimated that more than 2 million Haitians live abroad. Countries such as the United States, Canada and France are among the main destinations of Haitian when they left Haiti. Haiti's neighbors have had some positive impacts as well as some negative impacts. When put in the balance, the diaspora has been more beneficial to Haiti than negative. I can take myself as an example. I was born in Anse A Foleur, North West, Haiti and I was raised in Port Au Prince. I moved to the Bahamas where my parents used to live and later on settled in Miami. In Miami, I managed to graduate High School and go to college in Virginia. I have a bachelor's degree in Interdisciplinary Studies and a social science license from Florida Department of Education. This book is my first. If I was not in the Diaspora, it would be very difficult for me to achieve this academic success. I can put it in another way, if my parents did not sacrifice so much to move to the Bahamas and later on to the United States, it would be very difficult for me to do so.

The amount of research I have made in the United States would have been almost impossible to make in Haiti. I have examples of people that have achieved the American Dream in all kind of fields. The same history is happening in a lot of other countries where the Haitian Diaspora is present. The Haitian diaspora has learned so much outside of Haiti, they really want to go back to Haiti and help. I am in the field of social science. I have learned a lot in that field. Once I finish this book, my dream is to talk about it wherever Haitian lives so they can understand how to fix the system in Haiti. A lot of other Haitians in other fields all over the globe are doing the exact same thing. Recently, the debate has been: should Haitians in Haiti run the country or should Haitians in the Diaspora run the country? My answer is Both. If Haiti is fixed, the Haitians in Haiti are able to take their own destiny in Hands with the support of the Diaspora. If Haiti is fixed, the diaspora with the large sum of knowledge it has acquired outside of the country can make a huge difference besides sending money. At the same token, if the system remains the same with all its weakneses, the Haitians in Haiti will not be able to do much and the diaspora will not be able to do much.

When Michel Joseph Martelly became president, a lot of people in his administration came from the Diaspora. It seemed to me he had a strong will to change things. The reality is, the same dysfunctional system is there. As long as the same dysfunctional system is there, progress will be a dream not a reality. The same system that was preventing other presidents in Haiti from developing the country, is the same system that was preventing Martelly from doing a good job. You see, in some ways, the system has a lot to do with the present predicament of the country. The word system here means, the broken institutions of the country. Not the international community, not the mulattoes, not the Haitians of Syrians and Lebanese origins, not the economic elite. Until the system is changed or until the institutions are fixed, the diaspora has to keep doing what it does best: sending money to Haiti and supporting its families with hard work and pride.

The Caribbean

A lot of Haitians are living in the neighboring countries such as the Bahamas, Dominican Republic and Puerto Rico. Even though these people have plans to move to the United States, Canada and France, a lot of times, things do not work out the way people think and therefore, they end up staying in the Caribbean for years before returning to Haiti or move to North America or Europe. The first people to migrate to the Caribbean were political leaders who were fleeing political instability in Haiti. In 1843, Jean Pierre Boyer escaped political instability in Haiti as president and went to Jamaica and later on to France where he finished his days. President Jean Bertrand Aristide escaped political instability in Haiti went to Jamaica and later on to Africa in the Coup D'etat that toppled his government in 2004. What I am trying to say here is that, the Caribbean has been there for us in political chaos and economic chaos.

There is a tendency that claims that the people in the Caribbean do not like Haitians. I disagree. They do not like the way we move into their countries because they have laws and regulations but they do like us. I used to live in the Bahamas where a lot of Haitians are still living. The Bahamas is a small country with a booming tourism, banking and service industries. The Bahamian government arrested Haitians when there is a new boat coming to the country. Whenever the Haitian government does its part in controlling the people in Haiti in preventing them from living the country, the Haitians already settled in the Bahamas have some peace of mind. Whenever a new boat arrived, there is concerned about the status of Haitians living illegally in the Bahamas. Some estimated the number of Haitians living in the Bahamas to be more than 40 thousand. I am not here discussing about the accuracy of that number. All I know is that, there is a growing number of Haitians living in the Bahamas. Even though there is strong discrimination, the fact of the matter is people have a common history. After people have lived in a region for decades, they start developing a common culture.

Another example I have about Haitians living in the

Caribbean is the Dominican Republic. A lot of Haitian students are in the Dominican Republic studying in all kind of fields. Some went to DR just to work and not to study. Me and my wife spent 2 weeks in Dominican Republic. I visited Santiago and Moca. Both cities are beautiful cities. The country is very beautiful and organized. There is a large number of Haitians living in the Dominincan Republic. Some estimated that the number of Haitians living in the Dominican Republic to be more than 1 million. Some groups claim that the number is higher than 1 million. I am not here discussing numbers and statistics. One thing is for certain is the fact that, there is a growing number of Haitians living in the Domincan Republic. What about Cuba? Cuba has been there for Haiti in the thick and thin. The Cubans doctors are all over the country helping us with our state of health. A growing number of Haitians live in Cuba. Some are working, some are in school and some are just visiting family members. I have not yet visited Cuba. My goal is to visit Cuba whenever I have the chance to do so.

There are other countries in the Caribbean where Haitians are living that I do not mention because I cannot mention every countries so I can keep the book and this chapter shorter. Even though the Haitian diaspora has been helpful to us in Haiti, only a stable government will make the great contribution that supposes to happen, happen in the lives of the Haitian people. The fact of the matter is: the Haitian population is increasing at an alarming rate. The government has to be organized to create a state of economic prosperity for all Haitians. There is a tendency that the countries in the Caribbean have to do more to help us. While this may be politically correct. They want to help us but we have to meet them at some point. The more we can do to create political stability, the more they will be able to do to help. The January 12, 2010 earthquake has proven that they want to help us. The Caribbean nations or the CARICOM nations were among the first to arrive in Haiti in helping the victims of the earthquake.

The United States

The United States has one of the largest concentration of Haiti in the Disapora. The Haitian diaspora in the United States can be seen as the center of the Haitian diaspora worldwide. The city of Miami is considered by many as the capital of the Haitian diaspora worldwide. Some Haitians in the Diaspora in the United States are famous. Others are not. People such as Jean Baptiste Point Du Sable and W.E. B. Dubois are very well known. Jean Baptiste Point Dusable is well known as the founder of the city of Chicago. Chicago is the third largest city in the United States based on the 2012 facts. In 1968, the city and the state recognize Jean Baptiste Point Dusable as the founder of the city. WEB Dubois was born in Massachussets from Haitian parents. He was instrumental in the creation of NAACEP and in the advancements of freedom for all people. The National Association for the Advancement of Colored People has been in existence since 1901.

That organization has been very influential in advancing the agenda of people of color before 1901 to the civil rights movements of the 1960s. After the civil rights movements of the 1960s, the NAACP is still standing in advancing the agenda of the Black people. The NAACP witnessed Barack Hussein Obama becoming the first black president of the United States. In 2001, the Bush Administration nominated Pierre Richard Prosper as the ambassador at large for war crimes. Pierre Richard Prosper was born in Denver, Colorado and was raised in Upstate, New York. He was born in the United States from Haitian parents. Kwame Raoul was born in Chicago from Haitian parents. He replaced president Barack H. Obama in his senate seat in Illinois. There are countless examples of Haitians doing well and good in the United States.

The state of New York has a large Haitian population. Besides Florida, New York has one of the oldest Haitian community in the United States. Most of these Haitians who settled in New York escaped the Duvalier dictatorship. It is believed that over 7 hundred thousand Haitians are living in different cities in New York. In New York, cities such as Harlem, Brooklyn, queens and Manhattan have large number of Haitians.

In Florida, there is a growing community of Haitians all over the state. Cities such as Miami where I live and where I graduate high school has one of the largest community of Haitians in the Diaspora. It is estimated that over 2 hundred thousand Haitians live in the city of Miami alone. Again, this number here may not be accurate. I am not here discussing numbers and statistics. Phillip Brutus, Ronald Brise, Jean Monestime among others have represented the Haitian community in the city of Miami with pride. Cities such as Fort Lauderdale, Delray Beach, Palm Beach, Orlando and many others in Florida have large Haitian communities that are progressing as the nation progresses and also these Haitians communities have set back when things are not going on well in the country.

In the United States, other cities such as: Atlanta, Chicago, Philadelphia, Washington, DC, Detroit, New Jerseys and many others have large community of Haitians that are progressing at an alarming rate. Like the American preachers like to say, you are not waiting on God, God is waiting on you. The Haitian Diaspora has to stop waiting for things to get better in order to assist Haiti. We have to be organized enough to make things better for Haiti. The Diaspora has the knowledge and the money but there is no organization to change things or make things better in Haiti. The time has come for the Diaspora to organize itself in a serious way without giving excuses and playing the victim.

Canada

In North America, the Haitian community in Canada is one of the strongest and also it is one of the most successful. Canada has been a fascinating country to me because of the quality of its institutions. Quite frankly, in making research to write this book, Canada has been one of the best examples among a lot of other countries that I have made my research on. In the 1960, less than 40 thousand people from Haiti were living in Canada. Today the Haitian diaspora in Canada is more than 100 thousand according to a lot of researchers. Again, I am not here discussing numbers or arguing about statistics. The key thing here is to know that there is a growing number of Haitians living in Canada and their contribution to Haiti is enormous. Just like in the United States, Haitians in the 1960s were fleeing the dictatorship of Francois Duvalier and found a way to settle in Canada particularly in the French speaking region of Quebec in the city of Montreal.

In the 1980s and 1990s, large number of Haitians started moving in the western region of Quebec that is Ontario. These Haitians started settling in cities such as Toronto and Ottawa. It is believed that more than 30 thousand Haitians live in the province of Ontario. People such as Michaelle Jean, Regine Chassagne, Luck Mervil among others are well known in the Haitian diaspora in North America and Haiti. No Haitian in the Diaspora has occupied a higher role in government than Michaelle Jean. She was born in Port Au Prince in 1957. She moved to Canada in 1968 with her parents at the age of 11. The family settled in the city Thetford Mines, Quebec. Because of family issues, Jean's mother later on moved with her along with her sister in Montreal. She was educated at the University of Montreal where she received a bachelor of arts and went on to study in several universities in Europe. She speaks several languages including Italian.

In 1988, she became a reporter, filmmaker and broadcaster for Radio Canada. Michaelle Jean is married with Canadian filmmaker Jean Daniel Lafond and the couple has an adopted daughter from Jacmel, a city in Haiti. Michaelle Jean was appointed governor of Canada by Queen Elizabeth II of the United Kingdom on the recommendation of the former prime minister of Canada Paul Martin in 2005. While in office, she attended the inauguration of President Rene Preval for a second term in 2006. In 2008, she left Europe before time to settle parliamentary dispute in the government of Canada. In 2009, she welcomed president Barack H. Obama to Canada for a state visit. Michaelle Jean stepped down from being the governor of Canada in 2010.

Before Michaelle Jean departure, the United Nations already had plans for the former governor. The officials in the United Nations named her special envoy to Haiti. Her foundation known as the Michaelle Jean Foundation focus on promoting education, culture and creativity among youth from rural, northern and poor communities in Canada. Michaelle jean truly has made the pride of the Haitian diaspora in North America and the haitian people in Haiti.

France

The relationship between France and Haiti is Unique because of the history of the two countries. The treaty of Ryswick in 1697 gave France the opportunity to have the western part of Saint Domingue as colony from Spain. Ever since then, the influence of French culture, tradition and norms has been present in the country. In the early days of the republic, the people of Haiti never move to France with the goal of creating a community. Toussaint Louverture, Jean Pierre Boyer, Jean Claude Duvalier and many other Haitian politicians moved to France because they were fleeing political instability in Haiti. Jean Claude Duvalier was born in Port Au Prince from President Francois Duvalier and Simone Ovide Duvalier in 1951. Early in his life he attended the College Bird and Institution Saint Louis De Gonzague, two famous private high schools in Port au Prince, Haiti.

In 1980, he married Michele Bennett Pasquet. The marriage produced two children: Nicolas Duvalier and Anya Duvalier. Jean Claude Duvalier became president in 1971 and left power for France in 1986. Early on in France, Jean Claude Duvalier lived the good life because of the money he had on his bank account. He applied for political asylum and was denied by the French government. As far as the French government was concerned, giving asylum to Duvalier means that, other politicians can terrorize their people and seek refuge to France. The French government was not violating international laws in not giving Jean Claude Duvalier asylum. The government was trying to set a good example for leaders in other countries that think, they can terrorize their people and then just escaped with the money and their family to European countries. As of 2012, the international community has been more careful in helping dictator flee their countries.

In the 1980s and 1990s, some European countries would accept a dictator to settle there and live a peaceful life. In the 21st century, this policy has changed. No safe haven for dictators in the industrialized world. Jean Claude Duvalier went to France in seeking political asylum. Other Haitians went to France to study and return to Haiti. Some finish their study and return to France, some finish their study and stay in France. Just like here in North America, there is a growing Haitian community in France. They are involved in local politics, in Education, health care and a lot of other fields. Jean Leopold Dominique, Herve Telemaque, James Noel among others have made the pride of the Haitian diaspora in their respective field of study. Unlike Haitian communities in the English speaking world or the Spanish speaking world, the Haitian community in France is unique because of the cultural attraction that remain the same. The urgency to help Haiti in an institutional way is very strong in the mind of the educated elite in France.

Just like the Haitian communities in other countries, they are waiting for the government of Haiti to stabilize the country so they can give their contribution. The best thing to do is not to wait but to act by organizing themselves. If sending money to family members in Haiti was enough, the country would not have been in this current situation. While all the indications prove that progress has been made in the Haitian diaspora in France from the 1960s and onward, the country has gone backward. What happens? Well, the institutions are weak. I mean they are very weak. The potentiality of the Haitian diaspora in France by itself is strong enough to strengthen the government in Haiti to do better in creating the required environment for the diaspora to give its participation in the country. While the Haitian diaspora in Miami has given me strength and hope to write this book, the Diaspora in France has given me optimism. The Haitian community in France used to play, is playing and will play a significant role in the rebuilding of a better Haiti for all Haitians.

South America

This chapter would be incomplete if we forget about the Haitian Diaspora in South America primarily in Brazil and Chile. It is estimated almost 400 thousand Haitians live in South America primarily in Brazil and Chile. These people are a great economic help for Haiti and should organize themselves to Help Haiti. The government of Haiti is so broken, we cannot wait in the Diaspora for things to get better to help. We have to organize ourselves so well that we will force things to get better. There are Haitian Diasporas in other parts of the world that are not mention in this book and they are doing a great job in helping their families in Haiti and helping their respective cities and countries where they live.

CHAPTER 15

THE INTERNATIONAL COMMUNITY

The relationship between the international community and Haiti has been a very complex one. Intellectuals, political scientists, politicians and the common people of Haiti have different point of views. The people that are against the international community involvement in the affairs of Haiti express themselves in a way that should be respected. The people that are for the involvement of the international community in Haiti have good reasons behind their position. The purpose of this last chapter of this book, is not to defend one side against another but to present the situation in such a way that, you can see why what happens in Haiti happens. I will never forget the earthquake in Haiti during January 12, 2010. The Haitian people by themselves were helpless during that time. More than 40 countries intervened directly and indirectly to support the Haitian people.

They come with financial and other kind of aids that prove to us that, we were not alone. The countries that did not send their planes to Haiti, donated whatever they have to international organizations such as the United Nations and World Health Organization to help Haiti. After the earthquake, billions and billions were pledged to help Haiti in overcoming that difficult time. While a lot of Haitians intellectuals are criticizing institutions such as the World Bank and the International Monetary Fund for the lack of economic support for Haiti, without strong institutions, these organizations cannot do much. You see, money is not the problem, practical ideas to take Haiti out of this mess is the problem. If the international community is going to come up with the money, we have to come up with the good ideas necessary for the country to go forward. So far, based on what I have seen, the government, under the leadership of president Jovenel Moise and past presidents is unable to come up with the necessary ideas that can help Haiti get out of this present predicament.

While I am not here defending the International institutions, I am sure they want to help us. The truth of the matter is: we have to meet them at some point. They are not going to do everything for us. They are not going to dictate to us how to organize the political parties, the permanent electoral council, how many terms a president or a prime minister should have. They are not going to do that for us. All they are going to do, is to make suggestion, hoping that we listen to their suggestions and create our own destiny. The people who blame the international community the most, do not understand that, the government has a role to play. The international community and Haiti are a team. We have to pass each other the ball. When the IMF gives money to the leaders of Haiti, that is passing the ball. When the government implements a successful program, that is passing the ball back to the IMF. The world is globalized. The world is becoming a smaller place on a daily basis. I love the saying of the International Business Machine. Here I am talking about the US corporation, IBM. The saying says, solutions for a small planet. To the engineers at IBM, the world is a very small place. That is so true. With stable government, developing nations such as Haiti can accomplish things that were impossible before globalization.

The powerful Germans and Japanese corporations are private. If the government is ready to pay them to build a good airport in Haiti, they are going to build it. If the government is going to pay them to build a good soccer stadium in Haiti, they are going to build it. The only thing is that, the government has to be stable enough to see the project through. What I mean by that is continuity of government. One government should continue the project of another government. So, with globalization, the international community is an advantage for the countries that can create the necessary institutions and a disadvantage for the countries that cannot create the necessary institutions to see progress flowing.

CARICOM

Caricom or the Caribbean Community was founded in 1973 by four nations: Jamaica, Barbados, Guyana and Trinidad and Tobago. Caricom replaces the Caribbean Free Trade Association that was founded in 1958 to provide free trade between the countries that speak English in the Caribbean. Today about 15 countries are members of

Caricom plus 5 associate members and 7 observer nations. The treaty of chaguaramas started the Caribbean Community and Common Market in 1973 in Trinidad. Haiti became a member of Caricom in 2002. Our neighbor in the East, here I am talking about the Dominican Republic is not a full member of the organization. I do not know why a such regional country as the Dominican Republic is not a full member of the organization. Well, it is not up to me to decide. It is up to the governing committee of Caricom to decide what is going to happen to the membership of Dominican Republic.

During the Coup D'etat in 2004 against President Jean Bertrand Aristide, Caricom was very helpful in helping the country. The member countries of the organization condemned the coup and wanted the president to return to power as soon as possible. Unfortunately, that did not happen. The organization proved its stand on democracy in defending Haiti. I did not support the fact that Caricom suspended the status of Haiti in 2004. It was something internal not external. It is true that there was a coup in Haiti. I do not think that the coup gave Caricom the power to disqualify the membership of Haiti in the organization. It is not like per say, Haiti invaded a member country of the organization or Haiti does not comply with the rules of the organization. By rejecting the membership of Haiti in the organization in 2004, I think the member countries of Caricom had made things worst. With the arrival of the presidency of Rene Preval in 2006, good relationship between Caricom and Haiti has been restored.

Modeled after the European Union, the organization is

creating a lot of institutions to make its work more efficient in the Caribbean. The Caribbean Court of Justice is there to maintain peace between member countries over issues such as trade, corrupt leaders and so on so forth. The single market of Caricom is probably the most important reason why countries join the organization. However, the organization is being careful concerning the situation in Haiti and other countries. The countries with the strongest economy such as the Bahamas and Trinidad and Tobago do not want illegal workers to invade their territories for jobs opportunity. That is one issue right now between Caricom and Haiti. The political instability in the country makes it very difficult for us to take advantage of the opportunities that Caricom give.

Twelve of the fifteen members of Caricom are using the Caribbean Community passport. The only countries that have yet to use the passport are: Haiti, Bahamas and Montserrat. Currently there are strategies underway to have a Caribbean stock exchange similar to the New York Stock exchange. When that happens the way the politicians want it to happen, it will be a great step in the right direction. The Caribbean is of the most peaceful region in the world. The integration of Haiti in Caricom is good business for us and them.

African Union

The African union is a continental organization of 55 member states. With a population of over 1 billion people and a lot of natural ressources, good relationship between Haiti and the African Union is very important. Africa is the motherland. This is our root. The African Union is moving forward with a lot of investment from People's Republic of China and the European Union. I am publishing this book during the Corona Virus Crisis. This disease originated from China. A lot of countries in Africa are expelling Chinese citizens because they are frustrated with the virus. Good relationship between China and Africa is key for both Side. Haitian intellectuals used to go to West Africa and teach there. In Haiti, we have so much that we can learn from the African Union that can make the country better for all Haitians living outside and living inside. Haiti has been an observer since 2012. I think this is a good deal. I believe membership should be reserve only to countries in Africa. Even though Haiti is not a full member, we can still enjoy all the economic and cultural benefits that come from this great continent, our motherland Africa.

People's Republic of China and Haiti

For the last 30 years, People's Republic of China has been trying to have good relationship with Haiti. This search for good relationship between Haiti and Mainland China has not been successful because of the lack of vision of Haitian Politicians. This good relationship is more beneficial for Haiti than it is for China. More than 80% of the world countries have good relationship with mainland China. I do not understand why we are behind. Some people are blaming the United States. The question you have to ask yourself is that, why the US does not block the rest of the world and the Caribbean in having good relationship with China? I understand that the Corona Virus is going on now in 2020.

This virus should not stop the real politicians and the real intellectuals of the country in pushing for good diplomatic relationship with mainland China. The Chinese are investing billions and billions of dollars all over the Caribbean and Haiti can benefit from that massively.

NAFTA

NAFTA or the North American Free Trade Association is one of the largest geopolitical organization in the world. Since Haiti is part of the Caribbean which is part of North America, progress in NAFTA is progress for Haiti. We will not participate in this progress without creating the necessary institutions for the country to go forward. A lot of us think or wait for things to get better in other countries and invite their leaders to come and talk to us. While there is nothing wrong with that, we have to create the necessary institutions for the country to go forward. When you understand politics, you will realize that, the war between developed countries and developing countries are over institutions. The war is not over which one has more people or a greater army. It is about which one has the best system of government. It is about which one has the best educational system.

NAFTA was created in 1992 by the leaders of Canada, the United States and Mexico. The main reason for the organization as the name suggest is better trade with these three nations. George H W Bush, Brian Mulroney and Carlos Salinas agreed to form the organization. The early challenge was for the parliament in Canada, Mexico and the United Congress to agree with it. With a lot of works, the parliaments of these respective countries agreed for NAFTA. NAFTA decreases the fee in trade between Mexico and the United States. It was not a problem for Canada since trade between Canada and the United States did not have any fee or tariffs on it. The agreement has opened the three countries as if they were one. United States for example has had trade deficit with Canada and Mexico in the past because of better institutions in these two countries. Institutions or good governments have a lot to do with the future of trade between nations.

NAFTA is very good for Haiti. Once the government of Haiti reforms the necessary institutions to maintain the development of the country, free trade between NAFTA and CARICOM are good for both sections. You have to understand that NAFTA sees CARICOM as its backyard. This means, CARICOM and NAFTA are one. This is an alliance of over 16 trillion dollars. The Caricom economy is over 90 billion dollars. Even though the Dominican Republic is not part of Caricom, its economy is over 90 billion dollars. This means the economy of the Caribbean is over 180 billion dollars. How are we going to get our share in this pizza? The answer is simple: institutions. Haiti is not going to get better because of the size of the economy in North America. Haiti is going to do better because of the efficiency of its institutions. The country is located in one of the best region in the world. It is our responsibility to create or to reform the necessary institutions for progress to flourish.

OAS

The Organization of American States was one of the primary organization involved in Haiti after the January 12, 2010 earthquake. The countries of the Americas were present in Haiti in the name of that organization and the respective governments. In January 2012, the permanent council of the organization called for the international community primarily the members of the OAS to re-focus and re-think its aid to Haiti. The council understands that coordination can make a great difference in the livelihoods of the Haitian people. The officials of the council believe if the international community is really serious about Haiti, it must show that after this devastating earthquake that took the livelihood of more than 300 thousand people.

On June 2012, Prime minister Laurent Lamothe gave a speech to the general committee of the OAS in regard to what the Haitian government is expecting from the OAS and what the OAS should expect from the haitian government. To the prime minister, it is a partnership. It is a partnership where the organization works with Haiti and Haiti works with the organization. The future of the country is somewhat intertwined in OAS. The OAS works with NGOs and the Haitian government in different fields such as health care, education, entrepreneurship, etc. The job of the organization in Haiti is to see a better future for all Haitians. According to the leadership of the OAS, Haiti should be one more time the pearl of the Caribbean.

The first person to envision an organization where all the countries in the Americas can sit down and discuss the common issues where Simon Bolivar in 1826. As you probably know, Simon Bolivar is considered as one of the greatest leaders in South America. Countries such as Colombia, Bolivia, Peru and others, are free today because of the work of this man. To add on the ideas of Simon Bolivar, in the 1930s president Franklin Delano Roosevelt organized an Inter-American conference in Buenos Aires. One of the main reason for that conference was to discuss the shaping of the future OAS. Today the organization is one of the most powerful in the world and in the Region. In the 21st century Americas, the mission of the organization is to promote peace and security on the continent, good government, find common grounds when there is dispute among member states, eradicate poverty, etc. Every year, the organization has its general assembly in a different member state. In 2005, it was in Fort Lauderdale, Florida, USA.

Just like the other members, if Haiti is going to profit from the help of the OAS, reforms in the institutions of the country have to be a reality. The Haitian government has to meet the OAS at some point of balance. If they are going to help us with money, we have to have our ideas together. The country is in a constitutional period or constitutional crisis. That must be addressed before the help of the OAS can be felt by the Haitian population.

EU

The European Union is the third largest donor of Aid to Haiti behind the United States and Canada. After the earthquake of January 12, 2010, several conferences were held in several cities in Europe particularly in Madrid, Spain and Paris, France to help Haiti. More than 1 billion dollars were pledged by the European Union to Help Haiti recover after that tragedy. You have to understand, this is money pledged by the European Union, not the countries of the European Union. There are many other ways that the countries of the European Union pledged their money in Haiti. The EU is just one way among many that the respective countries of Europe give money to Haiti. The history of the European Union goes back as early as the 19th century.

The moves to create strong European institutions to unite Europe in a concrete way, really started in the first half of the 20th century. In 1957 the treaty of Rome was signed for better integration in the European coal and steel industries. The Treaty of Rome created the European Economic Community. In 1993, the European Economic Community was replaced by the European Union by the treaty of Maastricht, Netherlands. After working on a common currency for years, the Euro was introduced in 2002 as the currency of 12 European countries. Today, the European Union has about 27 member countries. Each one of these countries want to have the euro. They are working as hard as they can to join the Euro. Being a member state in the European Union does not mean you are automatically qualified to join the Euro. A country has to meet the economic requirements to join the Euro. Today, the European Union is one of the most important geopolitical institution on the planet. Politically, economically and socially, the European Union is a great model for Haiti.

The relationship between the European Union and Haiti is there to stay. That relationship is good for both parties primarily for Haiti because of the financial and political situations of the country. Just like I have mentioned countless of times in this book, without institutional reforms in the country, Haiti will not be able to enjoy the help that the European Union diplomats are passionate to give to the country.

UN

The coup d'Etat of September 30, 1991 paved the way for the official enter of the United Nations in Haiti. After the American Occupation in 1915 to 1934, most Haitians if not all did not want the presence of foreign troops in the country. Just like political instability made it possible for the American occupation, political instability made the presence of the United Nations possible in the country after that coup d'etat that was a nightmare for the Haitian people. The world is a global village. No country is really an island. We need one another and we depend on one another. The best way to keep the foreign troops outside of the country is to create a stable government. If that government is not there, the international community has to be involved. This is the way it is. Germany was not behaving well during the early years and the middle of the 20th Century. What happened? Well, the treaty of Paris punished them harshly during World War I and they were divided into four pieces during World War II.

My point here is that, if there is political instability, the world has to be involved. They have to be involved not only in Haiti but anywhere else. The Clinton Administration returned president Aristide to power in 1994 and ever since, the United Nations has been present in the country. The United Nations was very instrumental in keeping Aristide in power for the remaining months of his presidency in 1994. Under President Preval, things started to be normal and peaceful in 1995. Just like during his first term in office, Jean Bertrand Aristide was not able to finish his second term in office as president in 2004 because of another coup d' Etat. The United Nations was forced to enforce its presence in Haiti during that period onward. The United Nations has worked with different governments in maintaining the peace. Elections in Haiti is one of the most complicated period in the country.

If the presence of MINUSTAH was not in the country, recent elections such as the 2006 general election to elect Rene Preval for his second term and the 2010-2011 election to elect Michel Joseph Martelly as president could have been a nightmare for the Haitian people. Created on the history of the League of Nations after the second world war by the leaders of the world including Franklin Delano Roosevelt, the United Nations is the most important political organization in the world. I think the United Nations should remain in Haiti until we prove we can govern ourselves and make democratic elections without confrontation. The Haitian government has to create or to reform the necessary institutions to stabilize the country and therefore make the departure of the United Nations from Haiti as a democratic process not a forceful one.

CONCLUSION

This book gives you the basic information you need to know in order to make up your mind regarding the current situation in Haiti and what can be done about it. While it is clear that other countries and International organizations have played a significant role for Haiti to be in this predicament, the only way out is for us to put away the victim mentality and take full responsibility in the rebuilding and the reforming of the institutions of the country. This idea where poverty, peace, insecurity and prosperity of any country is related to its institutions is shared by university professors such as Daron Acemoglu and James Robinson. For the institutional rebuilding and reforming of the country, the different elites (Intellectual, political, economic, religious, medical, scientific, sportive, cultural, etc.) have to do their parts without giving excuses and blaming each other.

REFERENCES

Robert Heinl (1996). Written in Blood: The Story of the Haitian People, 1492–1995. Lantham, Maryland: University Press of America.

The 1805 Constitution of Haiti, May 20, 1805. Translation. From Webster University Faculty. http://faculty.webster.edu/corbetre/haiti/history/earlyhaiti/1805-const.htm (Accessed 4/30/18).

Hans Schmidt (1971). The United States Occupation of Haiti, 1915–1934. Rutgers University Press. p. 99. ISBN 9780813522036.

Popkin, Jeremy. You Are All Free: The Haitian Revolution and the Abolition of Slavery. (Cambridge University Press; 2010)

Girard, Philippe. The Slaves Who Defeated Napoléon: Toussaint Louverture and the Haitian War of Independence (Tuscaloosa: University of Alabama Press, November 2011).

Laguerre, Michel S. Diasporic citizenship: Haitian Americans in transnational America (Springer, 2016).

Maram, Mazen (7 February 2013). "Nigerian Biggest Opposition Parties Agree to Merge". Bloomberg. Retrieved 11 February 2013.

Duverger, Maurice (1964). Political Parties: Their Organisation and Activity in the Modern State (3 ed.). London: Methuen. p. 60-71.

Ware, Alan (1995). Political parties and party systems. Oxford University Press. p. 22.

Hicken, Allen (2009). Building party systems in new democracies. Cambridge University Press.

Robert Allen Rutland, The Democrats: From Jefferson to Clinton (U. of Missouri Press, 1995) ch. 1–4.

Whitaker, Reginald. The Government Party: Organizing and Financing the Liberal Party of Canada, 1930–1958 (1977)

Bell, David Scott, and Byron Criddle. The French Socialist Party: The emergence of a party of government (1988)

Belpolitik.com. "The Haitian Constitution Archived 2011-05-23 at the Wayback Machine." Accessed 9 Feb 2011

Chierici, Rose-Marie Cassagnol. Demele: 'Making It': Migration and Adaptation among Haitian Boat People in the United States (AMS, 1980).

"How the Westminster Parliamentary System was exported around the World". University of Cambridge. 2 December 2013. Retrieved 16 December 2013.

Linz, J. (1990). The perils of presidentialism. The journal of democracy, Volume 1(1), pp. 51-69.

Linz, J. (1985). Democracy: Presidential or Parliamentary does it make a difference. Connecticut: Yale university press

Duverger (1980). "A New Political System Model: Semi-Presidential

Brooks, Stephen (2007). Canadian Democracy: An Introduction (5th ed.). Don

"Role of the Court". Supreme Court of Canada. 23 May 2014. Retrieved 27 May2014

"Law 82-213 of 2 March 1982". Legifrance. Retrieved 2 August 2015.

"Ease of Doing Business in Haiti". Doingbusiness.org. Retrieved 24 January2017.

Hersher, Rebecca (5 October 2016). "Haiti's Presidential Election Delayed In Wake Of Hurricane". NPR. NPR. Retrieved 6 October 2016.

Vivien A. Schmidt, Democratizing France: The Political and Administrative History of Decentralization, Cambridge University Press, 2007, p. 22 Archived 2016-05-05 at the Wayback Machine, ISBN 9780521036054

Diana Conyers, "Decentralization: The latest fashion in development administration?" Archived 2014-05-22 at the Wayback Machine, Public Administration and Development, Volume 3, Issue 2, pp. 97–109, April/June 1983, via Wiley Online Library, accessed February 4, 2013.

Cardozo, Benjamin N. (1998). The Nature of the Judicial Process. New Haven: Yale University Press.

"United Nations Peacekeeping Operations". United Nations. 29 February 2016. Archived from the original on 23 March 2016. Retrieved 24 March 2016.

Levi, Edward H. (1949) An Introduction to Legal Reasoning. Chicago: University of Chicago Press.

Zelermyer, William (1977). The Legal System in Operation. St. Paul, MN: West Publishing.

Nelson, Dana D. (2008). Bad for Democracy: How the Presidency Undermines the Power of the People.

Minneapolis, Minnesota: University of Minnesota Press. p. 248. ISBN 978-0-8166-5677-6.

Sirota, David (August 22, 2008). "Why cult of presidency is bad for democracy". San Francisco Chronicle. Retrieved 2009-09-20.

Veser, Ernst (1997). "Semi-Presidentialism-Duverger's concept: A New Political System Model" (PDF). Journal for Humanities and Social Sciences. 11 (1): 39–60. Retrieved 21 August 2017.

Elgie, Robert (2 January 2013). "Presidentialism, Parliamentarism and Semi-Presidentialism: Bringing Parties Back In" (PDF). Government and Opposition. 46(3): 392–409. doi:10.1111/j.1477-7053.2011.01345.x.

Nousiainen, Jaakko (June 2001). "From Semi-presidentialism to Parliamentary Government: Political and Constitutional Developments in Finland". Scandinavian Political Studies

Carter, Byrum E. (2015) [1955]. "The Historical Development of the Office of Prime Minister". Office of the Prime Minister. Princeton University Press. ISBN 9781400878260.

Weaver, R. Kent (1985). "Are Parliamentary Systems Better?". The Brookings Review. 3 (4): 16–25. doi:10.2307/20079894. ISSN 0745-1253. JSTOR 20079894.

"Simon de Montfort: The turning point for democracy that gets overlooked". BBC. 19 January 2015. Retrieved 19 January 2015; "The January Parliament and how it

Zetter, Kim (26 September 2018). "The Crisis of Election Security". The New York Times. ISSN 0362-4331. Retrieved 20 August 2019.

Levin, Dov H. (June 2016). "When the Great Power Gets a Vote: The Effects of Great Power Electoral Interventions on Election Results". International Studies Quarterly. 60 (2): 189–202. doi:10.1093/isq/sqv016.

"Free and Fair Elections". Public Sphere Project. 2008. Retrieved 8 November2015.

Richard Bonney (1995), Economic Systems and State Finance, 680 pp.

David W. Conklin (1991), Comparative Economic Systems, Cambridge University Press, 427 pp.

Frederic L. Pryor (1996), Economic Evolution and Structure: 384 pp.

"The Organization of American States". Council on Foreign Relations. Council on Foreign Relations. Retrieved 12 November 2019

Kennedy, Paul (2007) [2006]. The Parliament of Man: The Past, Present, and Future of the United Nations. New York: Random House. ISBN 978-0-375-70341-6.

"4th African Union summit". January 2005. Archived from the original on 15 March 2008. Retrieved 29 September 2016.

ARTICLES BY ARCHANGEL DESHOMMES

Archange Deshommes has written more than 50 articles in French. He has written the articles on the Haitian crisis, current events such as the Trump presidency and other global topics. The articles have been published in online Haitian newspapers such as: Le Nouvelliste, Le National, Rezo Nodwes, etc. and Medium Articles in the USA. To read the articles or if you have any questions or comments, you can send him an Email at: Adeshommes@hotmail.com.

Here are some articles written by Archange Deshommes

1. Le système parlementaire de gouvernement: la seule solution durable à la crise politique actuelle en Haïti
2. Décentralisation politique et développement économique en Haïti
3. Covid-19 et la responsabilité des élites en Haïti
4. Covid-19, la diaspora haïtienne et Haïti: nous sommes une seule famille malgré la pandémie
5. Professeur Monferrier Dorval, Réformes constitutionnelle et institutionnelle en Haïti

6. George Floyd, le racisme systématique en Amérique et le silence de Jovenel Moise
7. L'Église en Haïti: la principale institution chargée de défendre la famille, la morale et de s'opposer à l'immoralité sexuelle
8. La nécessité de réformer le système de police en Haïti
9. La nécessité de réformer le système des tribunaux en Haïti
10. La nécessité de réformer le système pénitentiaire en Haïti

11. La nécessité de réformer les gouvernements des sections communales, départementale, et communale en Haïti
12. Élection directe et le danger du despotisme en Haïti
13. Le danger d'éliminer la langue française en Haïti
14. Résoudre les problèmes des gangs et restaurer la sécurité publique en Haïti
15. Le Core Group en Haïti: Ils ne vont pas reconstruire Haïti pour nous, nous devons le faire nous-mêmes.

16. Élections indirectes: la seule façon de résoudre la crise du CEP (Conseil Electoral Permanent) en Haïti
17. Avec élection indirecte ou régime d'assemblée: nous pouvons avoir la paix et la prospérité en Haïti
18. Avec les réformes politiques: le socialisme, le capitalisme et la privatisation fonctionneront tous en Haïti
19. Avec des réformes politiques: les plans quinquennaux peuvent fonctionner en Haïti

ABOUT THE AUTHOR

Archange Deshommes was born in Anse-à-Foleur, North West, Haiti and raised in Port-au-Prince, Haiti. He attended primary and secondary schools in Haiti, the Bahamas and Miami, FL, USA (Ecole Evangelique Nouvelle Jerusalem, Centre De Formation Emile Roumer and College Pythagore Haitien, Port Au Prince, Haiti) Bahamas Academy of the SDA (Seventh Day Adventist School) Nassau, Bahamas and North Miami Senior High School, North Miami, FL USA. He holds a bachelor's degree in interdisciplinary social sciences from Virginia State University and Norfolk State University in Virginia, USA. He is currently (2021) working on his Master's degree in Educational Leadership at Barry University in Miami, FL, USA. He is certified in Social Science by the Florida Department of Education. He was a teacher in Miami Dade County Public Schools. For 20 years he has been doing social science research mainly in governments such as: different types of governments, federal or national government, regional governments, municipal governments, etc. Different types of political systems, political regimes and democracies. He has also carried out research in government institutions such as the judiciary: (the judicial system or courts, the police system and the prison system). He has published more than 50 articles in

Some of the best known online newspapers in Haiti and the USA such as : Medium Articles, Le National, Le Nouvelliste, Rezo Nodwes, etc.

Adeshommes@hotmail.com

Printed in the United States
by Baker & Taylor Publisher Services